How the
French
Created
CANADA

From New France to French Canada

JULIE PERRONE

DRAGON
HILL

The Publisher: Dragon Hill Publishing Ltd.

Library and Archives Canada Cataloguing in Publication

Perrone, Julie, 1978–
  How the French created Canada / Julie Perrone.

Includes bibliographical references.
ISBN 978-1-896124-18-6

  1. Canadians, French-speaking—History. 2. French—Canada—
History. I. Title.

FC136.P47 2009   971'.004114   C2008-907397-5

ISBN 13: 978-1-896124-18-6

Project Director: Gary Whyte
Project Editor: Nicholle Carrière
Production: HR Media
Maps: Roly Wood
Cover Image: Photos.com

PC: 5

We acknowledge the support of the Alberta Foundation for the Arts for our publishing program.

CONTENTS

DEDICATION

To Chase, Caemon and Rob Lalonde

Acknowledgements

This book is a first experience for me, and for this I should extend my sincerest gratitude to Nicholle Carrière, who has helped me tremendously in this process. I should mention that while many have helped with the revision, if mistakes remain, they are mine only. Besides this professional encouragement, I would like to underline the indirect contributions of my families. The Perrones and Vinettes, for showing me how to be a true French Canadian, and the Lalondes and Dubies from Coniston and Sudbury, who showed me I should be proud of my roots and never take them for granted. Merrrrrrrrrrrrrci. And of course, my husband Rob should have his name in here, simply for supporting me, my overdramatic worries and my overly ecstatic moments. I love you more than anything in the world.

INTRODUCTION

This book will not solve a mystery. You will not be surprised by its general idea. In fact, you have already said in your head, before purchasing this book, that you know exactly how the French created Canada. They were the first ones here, you might say, which would be enough to demonstrate their influence on Canada. I thought it would be that easy, too. I was indeed a bit naïve when I began writing this book about how the French created Canada. As it is, my life is surrounded with examples of how the French have influenced, to this day, this beautiful country. I myself was raised in a French Canadian family. Growing up in Montréal, in the

French-speaking part of Verdun, I went to a French Catholic school where we said a prayer before the beginning of each day and reluctantly learned English as soon as grade four. I married a French Canadian from Northern Ontario, whose family is always proud to demonstrate that despite living in English Ontario, they still speak French, and very well, indeed. We have decided to raise our children in a French environment and are required by the government to send them to French school. So writing a book about the French influence on Canada should be easy, right? Not as easy as I thought.

When gathering the information for this book, I realized that this was a big task, for one reason—the French were and are part of the whole history of Canada. To show you the French influence in this country, I have to tell you about Canadian history as a whole. It is a big task, but I promised myself one thing— this book would *not* be a history book. First of all, because history books are sometimes boring and talk more about events than people, and about the big picture more than the little details. In this book, I want to show you these little details, to talk about some interesting people. Second, this book is not historical because some pieces are missing. The French have had a great influence on Canada, but not on everything. I am modest enough not to assume that we French have had a hand in absolutely everything Canadian.

The French started to shape our history right at its beginning, founding a colony in what is now the province of Québec. New France had a rocky existence and a short lifespan. In 1760, it was conquered by the British and eventually became Lower Canada, then Canada East, and then Québec. Two and a half centuries have passed since the Conquest, but the French language is still an official language throughout the country, even though a minority of Canadians actually speaks it (22.1 percent in the 2006 census). The French legacy is everywhere, from recipes imported by Norman and Briton ancestors, to Church architecture, with notorious men and women in between. Canada exists today partly because the French wanted to travel outside their European borders. They left their homeland, searching for a better way of life. The French have held onto their language, which is one of the foundations for developing an identity. This identity changes constantly and is different from one region to the next, but the French Canadian communities, wherever they may be, are a living example of the courage of our French settlers. These communities are, in a way, a *coup de chapeau* to Frenchmen Jacques Cartier and Samuel de Champlain, among other greats.

To look at how the French created Canada, I have to go back to the beginning of this country, even before Jacques Cartier set foot on the continent. *Les français* were the first Europeans here, and their traditions developed as the nation itself developed. By going this far back, the traces of what is French and what is not are easier to find. This is why the work was so hard in the first place—many of us are descendents of French settlers, but do we really know what comes from the French and what doesn't? Take typical French Canadian food, for example. With a bit of research, it is easy to find that our famed *cretons*, thought to be a purely French Canadian invention, are in fact from Normandy, a region from which a majority of the original settlers came. The New World settlers modified the recipe because they had to adapt to the resources available and, in the meantime, incorporated suggestions from the Natives. This example demonstrates how something such as *cretons* gets modified throughout its life, making its origins difficult to identify. The French have been here for so long that most of what they brought here— knowledge, methods or philosophies—evolved in different ways.

On another note, a book on the French influence in Canada could easily become a book about Québec, because it is the most obvious legacy of the French. But they have spread their influence everywhere in the country, and many traces of their passage can be found. More than a quarter of the French population lives outside the province of Québec, which means that Canada as a whole has to be examined. The stories of these communities are priceless to the French narrative and demonstrate that French Canada does not consist only of the province of Québec. Of course, there is no denying that *la belle province* is an important aspect of this book, but I chose to cover this as much, or as little, depending on your point of view, as every other community.

The Francophones of Canada have created different cultures, mostly because where they chose to live made them part of various histories. The history of the French on the Prairies is closely linked to that of the Métis people, often illustrated with Louis Riel and the formation of Manitoba. The Métis are descendents of French settlers who married Native women. Their history is, then, both that of French Canada and of the First Nations. The French in Ontario usually recall the school debate as a unifying time for them, fighting for the right to be educated in their mother tongue. A good number of Franco-Ontarians originally came from Québec, and they arrived in several waves, mostly because there was more work in Ontario than in overpopulated Québec. The province of Québec has the largest number of French

Canadians in the country, and it is the only province in which French is actually the official language. It was originally called New France, and the history of this place offers tales of conquest, rebellion, religious devotion, peaceful revolution and much more. For the Maritimes, it is the story of the Acadian deportation, the *Grand Dérangement*, that originally defined the culture. This history is peculiar because it includes people who now live everywhere in Canada and also in the United States (Maine and Louisiana for the most part) and France. Acadians are French Canadians because they speak French, although they have modified the language to a point where other French Canadians sometimes have trouble understanding them. French Canadians can be found in every part of the country, but you can see that these French communities are all very different.

Both the Government of Québec and the Catholic Church played an important part in the cultural survival of French Canadians in that province. We have been lucky in that sense; when two central institutions are on your side, it makes it easier to keep your culture and traditions alive. The French language remained in use in the province, thanks to initiatives from the government and the Church's stronghold on the educational system. Elsewhere, there was no supportive government and certainly no Catholic Church as powerful as that in Québec. But in other provinces, there were associations, gatherings of socially conscious Francophones wishing to secure their heritage by means of political pressure, militancy and diffusion of knowledge. These groups, formed by ordinary citizens, have consistently defended the rights of French minorities in other Canadian provinces, often without any official support and all the while fighting against discrimination. Associations lobbied for French education, which is why we can still talk about Canadian bilingualism today, why the French language is still relatively widely spoken and why French culture is ever so vibrant.

What is culture, first of all? Culture is often interpreted as a way of life, which might include religion, language, customs and beliefs. In short, culture is a vehicle for identity, meaning that by looking at a culture, we can somewhat understand the people. But what is this French culture, the French influence we can see in Canada? First and foremost, I think we ought to celebrate great French Canadians who have done so much for the nation. In the course of my history studies, we were often told not to focus on great men, as history was also made up of ordinary people. But the people who made Canada what it is were all, in a sense, ordinary Frenchmen, so some idea of what they have done and how it affects us today seems to be pertinent. French explorers, French settlers, French politicians—those are all the people we learned about in our history classes and about whom we perhaps don't want to hear any more. But we learn about them for a reason—they demonstrate how crucial the French were in the making of Canada. French influence is also represented in famous imports such as leisure activities or food. For this reason, the last part of the book is much less historical, as we examine some of the French customs and traditions still present in Canada.

As a historian, I know this work is incomplete. There are always debates about stories and their meanings, and I did not want to complicate things. As a French Canadian, I think the work is also incomplete—there could never be enough retelling of the great stories that contribute to creating the French identity. In reality, this book will always be a work in progress, simply because history is constantly being rewritten and is endlessly moving forward. So let's look at the coming pages as a "snapshot" of what the French influence looks like today.

CHAPTER ONE

JACQUES CARTIER, OR HOW THE FRENCH DISCOVERED CANADA

E urope's ego and consumption patterns became too much for the continent. There you have it. This summarizes why Europeans decided to explore the world and how they came to discover the Americas. They followed a simple marketing concept: once a particular market had been fully developed, in this case the European market, it was time to find a new one. Because most European countries could not offer new goods, they had to find new places to offer the same old goods—and find new trade items as well. European countries had been dealing with (that is, warring against) each other for centuries by then, and the products they sold to (that is, stole from) each other were always a) the same ones, and b) the same price. This was certainly not an exciting business world, and they needed to find a new world to break the routine of cabbage, potatoes and turnips.

France was not the first country to see the American land on the horizon. Rather, it was Christopher Columbus, on behalf of the Spanish government, who first stepped foot on the continent. He landed in the Bahamas and in Central America, finding islands that he thought were the Orient. Soon after, explorers Amerigo Vespucci, Vasco Núñez de Balboa and Ferdinand de Magellan, among others, were able to inform the world how wrong Columbus had been—the Orient had suddenly become the New World.

It wasn't until 1524 that France, led by Francis I, decided to take part in the exploration frenzy, mostly in the hope of finding a land filled with riches or, even better, a shortcut to the China Sea. Why China? For the many products the Chinese could offer that were not available in Europe, such as spices and silks. Apparently, our ancestors craved foods that actually tasted like something and fabric to make pretty harlequin pants. China was also a potential market for European goods, provided the Chinese developed a taste for turnip stew. Francis I was the first French king to embrace the Italian Renaissance, the movement that we associate today with great artwork and literary masterpieces. The king worked hard to bring this artistic movement to France, but his most important legacy, in the context of this book, is that he encouraged worldwide exploration.

Even if France has somewhat lost its global influence today, back then, the kingdom was a powerful one. France is the land of the Franks. A community that can be traced back to the third century, the Franks are said to bear the name of their weapon of choice, a spear whose name was *francisca* in Latin. Great kings ruled France, among them Dagobert, who figures in one of our playground songs: *Le bon roi Dagobert a mis sa culotte à l'envers* (The good king Dagobert put his underwear on inside out). Why we remember him for his underpants, I am not certain, but it makes him quite sympathetic, doesn't it? There was also Charlemagne, an individual whom I remember despising in primary school because we were taught that he was the one who had invented school. Not a good thing to say to kids who long to go play outside. It took me a while to forgive him, probably until I realized that schools had existed way before him, and that he had simply worked towards building an educational system that was available to larger populations. The French kings did not have much imagination when the time came to name their descendants. Because of this, it seems that nicknames were needed to differentiate each one from the next. We have Charles the Bald, Charles the Simple, Charles the Fat and Charles the Fair, but Louis was definitely the name of choice for France's rulers, accompanied by a telling comment about each king's style of ruling—the Stammerer, from Overseas, the Lazy, the Fat, the Lion, the Young, the Quarreller, the Prudent, the Great and the Just.

The French might have been unimaginative with their rulers' names, but they did rethink the way their world was going. France was home to the revolution of 1789 that changed the political world; it questioned the idea of kingdoms and suggested another source of power— the people. The American Revolution had taken place more than a decade earlier, but this rebellion did not seek to remove all the powers granted to the ruler of England. To the contrary, what Americans wanted was to be represented in the British government; in other words, to share the power, not take it away. The French Revolution really began because of a rise in the price of bread, a staple for most French families at the time. Expensive bread caused major discontent, just like the price of gas gets us going today. When a vital commodity ends up costing more, we always blame the government; the French seem to have been the first ones to do so. Maybe we inherited this trait from them...

What made things worse is that the bourgeoisie and the royalty could afford to buy and throw out as much food as they wanted, probably enough food to feed the whole country. This might have been a tad maddening for the people who were starving, but I'm no expert. The common people rebelled and ended up beheading their king, Louis XVI, who had tried to escape with his wife, Marie Antoinette. People were already pretty angry at their king, but to see him cowardly trying to escape the country, at night and disguised, probably did not help his case. To top it off, the French people had grown to hate Marie Antoinette, whose unfaithfulness was by then almost common knowledge.

A group took over to form a new government, and they decided that since the whole structure of the country had been changed, they might as well change everything else. This was perhaps not France's greatest moment, but it was a funny one—they made up a new calendar, with weird new names for the months (for example, Thermidor for July and Frimaire for November) and 10-day weeks. Taking a two-week vacation must have been a great way to celebrate... Needless to say, the French eventually went back to the calendar used by the rest of their neighbours. They struggled with their new status until one of the most famous kings in history, an emperor, actually, Napoleon

Bonaparte, staged a *coup d'état* in 1799 and took power as the first consul of France. Napoleon crowned himself emperor, which brought France back to square one—powerful but ruled by only one individual (a very short one). He conquered most of Europe in the name of France, codified its centuries-old laws and made hiding your hand in your jacket a very popular pose. It would be mortally boring to cover French law here, but suffice it to say that today, the province of Québec has a hybrid legal system that uses both French civil law and British common law.

Back to the time of exploration...France had by then won yet another war against England and was doing well. Which war, you might ask. My response would be...does it matter? The English and the French had started to hate each other in 1066, when a vassal of the French kings, William, Duke of Normandy, decided to take over the neighbouring kingdom of England. From that time until the French Revolution, the two nations fought over 30 different wars, one of which lasted 100 years. By the time France began to look overseas, the two nations had been fighting for most of their political existence. This could arguably be a possible source for the troubles Canada has experienced during its history.

In any case, France was in the best position it had been in for years and celebrated this with overseas exploration and the search for a faster waterway to China. Interestingly enough, the French kingdom's first mandated explorer was an Italian from Florence, Giovanni da Verrazano, who eventually reached New-foundland but didn't find a secret way to China. The French were at the vanguard of outsourc-ing, apparently. Following what was considered a commercial failure, Francis I waited 10 years, until 1534, before sending Jacques Cartier, an acquaintance, to explore the new continent.

Cartier, born in the town of St. Malo in Brit-tany, reached the North American continent in May 1534 after an "easy" three-week voyage. After exploring the area, he set up a cross at Gaspé on July 24 with *Vive le roi de France* written on it. Upon his return to France, the king decided to name the territory the Province of New France. Explorers and early colonists were really imaginative when it came down to naming new territories: New England, New York, New Hampshire, Nova Scotia. Then again, these were all in a New World, which could explain the pattern.

While the British took possession of entire nations through the "cunning use of flags," as comedian Eddie Izzard would say, the French planted crosses for the king, reminding them-selves of the sacred powers of their regent. Kings were believed to have been chosen by God and, curiously, He always chose the son of the previous king, an unintended coincidence, I am sure. In any case, kings were considered semi-gods and, consequently, they were always right.

Of course, politicians nowadays do not have the same advantage; instead, I think we always assume they are wrong. Devotion to the king was sincere back then, and claiming a piece of land in his name was only natural and demonstrated the pride in being French. Royalty was sacred in such a way that to speak ill of any royal was considered a crime—not only in France, but also in New France. In 1671, settler Pierre Dupuy spoke badly of the deceased King of England (I guess this was one of the years that France and Britain liked each other) and had to walk around without a shirt in February with a rope around his head, asking for forgiveness. Then he was branded with a *fleur de lys*. I think just standing there without a shirt would have been enough; the brand was probably not the worst thing, it may have actually warmed him up.

This flag up on a hill in Gaspésie was, then, the official beginning of Canada. If we were to be technical, a book with a title such as *How the French Created Canada* could end here, as the mystery has now been revealed. But, of course, the discovery of our future country is not the only great achievement of our French ancestors. They colonized the territory and imported a way of living, a culture and values that have endured since the time of Cartier. He was undoubtedly the first Frenchman to contribute to the creation of Canada, not only because he discovered it, but also because he was the first to draw a map of the St. Lawrence River. He made the existence of the valley "official" by writing down its physical information. During the years of exploration and conquest, before something was recorded on paper, it did not exist and, by extension, was not owned by anyone. Never mind the fact that Cartier probably had to ask some Natives to move over while he planted a cross dedicating this uninhabited land to a foreign power.

The remains of Cartier's first colony were found recently, or at least it is assumed the remains found belonged to him, and this rekindled interest in this Portuguese-speaking Frenchman. Indeed, Jean Charest, Québec premier, announced in 2006 that archeologists had unearthed burnt timber in Cap-Rouge, near Québec, that dated back to the 16th century, as well as fragments of a fancy plate also made around the same time. Apparently, this plate was so elaborate, archeologists can assert that it must have belonged to a French aristocrat, and there was only one aristocrat on the continent during this period—Roberval, who accompanied Cartier on his second voyage. A museum in St. Malo, a port city in Brittany in northwestern France, still displays fragments of one of the ships Cartier sailed to Canada—*La Grande Hermine*, *Le Petite Hermine* or *L'Emerillon*. Another special connection between our country and Cartier's hometown lives on in the form of the Transat Québec St. Malo, a boat race that takes place every four years. About 30 teams race across the Atlantic for approximately 14 days, braving storms and a severe lack of sleep.

During the time of exploration, St. Malo benefited tremendously from its situation, enriching itself from trade with Canada, and also from pirates—yes, pirates. This port city was no city of angels—it actually tried to secede from France because it considered itself neither French nor Breton, but pirate! Not many people know that French Canadians may have some pirate genes.

Although Canada was discovered in 1534, its exploration really began a year later, when Cartier returned with three ships and explored the Native villages of Stadacona and Hochelaga, which would eventually be "found" by others and given, respectively, the names of Québec City and Montréal. Apparently, a village only became a real place after it was discovered by a European.

Exploration became the focus of overseas voyages for France, as the nation was still trying to find a waterway to China within the new continent. Before that time, like most nations, France was looking for almost mythical locations that supposedly had jewels and gold everywhere. The idea was inspired by the Spanish, who had "discovered" the Mayan civilization and pillaged all of its riches. The rest of Europe hoped to be as lucky, which, of course, did not happen. Cartier was asked yet again to return to Canada to colonize the territory. Close to 400 men accompanied Cartier, but most of them returned to France with him right after the winter. Cartier had found what he thought was gold, so he rushed home to France to show the king his findings, instead of staying in Canada to establish a colony as he was supposed to. As it turned out, what Cartier brought was iron ore and quartz, which gave birth to the now classic expression: "False as a Canadian diamond," and made New France much less interesting.

Despite this mistake, Cartier's name is everywhere. In Québec alone, there is a river, a bridge and an island that keep the memory of Cartier alive. Not only this, the people on Cartier's ship have also left a legacy, their family names, which are still in evidence today. The Le Blancs, Hamels, Fleurys and Legendres of today's society owe their presence here to the French settlers that accompanied Cartier in his endeavours. Another of Cartier's legacies—he was the first to plant and grow crops in New France, namely cabbage, lettuce and turnips, which were staple foods in France at the time. Since these were not native to New France, it is Cartier who we should thank for bringing in these vegetables. That said, don't tell a kid that he should thank Cartier for the cabbage rolls he has to finish before getting dessert. Finally, Cartier was the first to write down the name of our future nation, though what he wrote down was the Iroquois term for "village." Our country is a village, a pretty big one, that is for sure. But beyond the village story that we have all learned in school, several other theories exist about how our nation got its name, and each seems more frivolous than the next. For example, two stories trace the name back to Spanish and Portuguese explorers, because in both languages *ca nada* means "here nothing." Apparently, this may have been said by disappointed discoverers to the Natives, who then repeated it to the French. I think the best story of all is that the name comes from a Frenchman, Cane, who tried to settle here but failed and left his name as a legacy. There is absolutely no proof to this story, but it was worth mentioning in the context of this book.

Another Frenchman had enough influence to survive the test of time. Louis Hébert has the honour of being known as the first "real"

European settler of New France, because as soon as he arrived on the continent in 1606, he began tilling a piece of land and tried to grow crops—this only two years after the founding of the colony. He was not the first settler to arrive in Canada, but the first one to actually settle and remain here for the rest of his life. Hébert landed in Port Royal and lived there for a while until he was given legal functions in Québec City, where he died. He had three children, and it was estimated by people from the Université de Montréal that by the 1800s, there were more than 4500 descendents of Hébert, suggesting that today there must be legions.

CHAPTER TWO

SAMUEL DE CHAMPLAIN, OR HOW THE FRENCH COLONIZED CANADA

The French created Canada by colonizing and exploring it. But how did this happen? Their only interest in the land up until then was to find a way to cross it to go somewhere else. One man, Samuel de Champlain, decided to make the colonization of Canada his life's goal. Another Frenchman who contributed immensely to the creation of Canada, Champlain was the son of a sailor and rose rapidly from being a member of a ship's crew to royal geographer, thanks to his previous voyages. The issue was raised that perhaps Champlain had never actually set foot on the continent he described so vividly, but that he in fact used written accounts from other people to his advantage. Either way, his well-delivered recollections were good enough to get him hired by the king. In 1604, he took part in colonization efforts in Acadia (Nova Scotia), which were close to disastrous. A couple of years later, he founded Québec City, and in the following years, he continued to explore the St. Lawrence River valley. Throughout his life, he kept going back to France to try to muster up some interest in (and funds for) the budding colony, with limited success.

Along with Pierre du Gua, Sieur de Monts, Champlain participated in the settlement of Acadia, the first colony of Canada. He first set up camp on Île Ste-Croix, and after a winter, moved to Port Royal, both in Nova Scotia. The first year was catastrophic—35 of the 79 inhabitants did not survive, either because of the rough winter on Île Ste-Croix or the abominable scurvy, which is why Champlain and du Gua decided to move the colony off the small island. This seems, in retrospect, to have been a good choice, since the colony developed well at Port Royal. The colony survived thanks in part to the revenues generated by a fur-trading monopoly that had been granted to du Gua for the territory. Once the monopoly was broken and people could bypass the colony's administration, the revenues stopped coming in and the colony dwindled but did not disappear. The territory was originally France's property, but it was only officially declared as such in 1632. It was taken over by British settlers in 1654, given back to France in 1667, under siege by its American neighbours a couple of times and ceded for good to Britain in 1713 with the signing of the Treaty of Utrecht. Acadia occupied an unfortunate geographical location—it was close enough to the British colonies that they wanted to conquer it but not profitable enough to the French to warrant its defence.

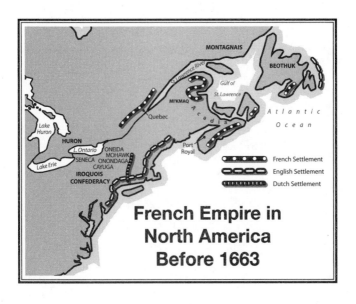

French Empire in North America Before 1663

After helping to found the first colony in Canada, Champlain went on to found Québec City in 1608. He wanted a post farther inland and closer to the Native population to have more control over the fur trade. In the first few weeks of Québec City's existence, Champlain narrowly escaped a murder attempt, a bad sign for the beginning of a new settlement. Champlain had uncovered a scheme to kill him that involved the colony's two locksmiths. The evil plan was obviously discovered in time, but the atmosphere in the colony was probably not pleasant for a while—people lived in mistrust, fear and resentment and had to deal with all this on empty stomachs and mouths full of scurvy. The attempted murder of Champlain was only a small step in an intricate plan of the Spanish, the Basques to be more precise, to take over the territory—such was the gruelling story that came out of the traitors' confessions. Some of the conspirators were returned to France with instructions to be sent to the gallows, while one was hanged and beheaded and his head put on a spike close to the colony as a message for those who tried to endanger the group of settlers. Apparently, Champlain did not appreciate traitors and really wanted his colonization idea to work.

Despite scurvy epidemics and constant fighting with the Natives, the colony endured and developed slowly. The remedy for scurvy was eventually obtained from the Natives (spruce beer, or anything with vitamin C), which probably helped the survival of the new nation and the smell of everyone's breath.

This paradise of healthy dentition lasted until the first, but short-lived, conquest of the colony by the British. The French and the British always fought in Europe, so settlers must not really have been surprised when the conflict continued overseas. In July 1629, privateers took over the territory of New France and claimed it in the name of Britain, which was at that time at war with France (surprise, surprise). For a few years in the early 17th century, then, New France was British. It was "conquered" by the Kirke brothers, who forced the capitulation of Champlain after a dreadful siege. The brothers cut off the supply line to the fortified colony, and soon the settlers were starving and Champlain had to surrender before people started killing each other for food. Champlain left New France in November 1629 and went to England, where he learned to his great surprise that the war between the two nations had been resolved before the conquest of his settlement. It took him three years to finally reverse the conquest on paper and take New France back for France.

Interestingly, all the trouble had been brought about by fellow Frenchmen—indeed, the Kirke brothers had been born in Dieppe, France, and simply sold their services to Britain (and laid waste to a colony peopled by their own). Of course, I never said that the French were all angels, but they did contribute to the history of Canada. The Kirke episode adds drama to our early history, so this should count for something, no? Good or bad, their actions were important enough that their name has survived for centuries.

In 2008, Québec City, Champlain's original colony, celebrated its 400th anniversary. The celebrations were mostly focused on the pride of keeping the tradition alive for 400 years, the tradition being...being French. The whole year was a celebration, from extreme skating in the heart of Old Québec to performances by Paul McCartney and Celine Dion on the Plains of Abraham. Important celebrations were also held back in 1908 for the Tercentenary—the most grandiose were probably the reenactments of life in New France and the conquest, as well as a royal visit to the city. While the celebrations of 1908 and those of 2008 were very different, they had one thing in common— British royalty was invited to both anniversaries, if we count Sir Paul McCartney as a member of the royalty. The City of Montréal was not able to celebrate as much for its 300th anniversary because the anniversary occurred during World War II—men were missing (and dying), and food and electricity were rationed. We have to look forward to 2042 to see what Montréal will do to celebrate its 400 years of existence.

Back to the Kirkes…The Kirke brothers were not the only delinquent French on the new continent. The aristocrats and the soldiers who immigrated to Canada were quite feisty and did not shy away from open conflict—they brought with them their love of fighting one another. In France, duels were all the rage, though they were frowned upon by the king, as demonstrated by the numerous edicts forbidding them. Some of the nobles who came to New France were involved in legal proceedings for their participation in duels and escaped to the colony to evade murder accusations. However, moving men from one place to another did not change their quarrelsome habits, and as early as 1646, a priest recorded the occurrence of a duel between two men working for the Ursulines, although no traces remain of the reasons for the duel or its end result. In the same story, the priest mentioned a duel between two French soldiers in Trois-Rivières in which one was injured and the other imprisoned. Some 20 years later, the first death by duel was recorded in New France, again one French soldier against another. The response here was a bit stronger than in France: the soldier who had won the duel was sentenced to death and hanged.

Duels back then were fought with swords, which meant the outcomes were rarely fatal—a death by duel was very dramatic and quite unexpected. Once the British took over the colony, duellers used pistols, which were much less forgiving (and probably not as entertaining to watch). If caught, duellers were punished. However, all the colonies were surrounded by deep, uncharted woods, and the constant threat of Native attacks kept people away from these unknown forests. Most duellers involved in a fight could easily escape colonial law by running into the woods and managing to never be found again. The inhabitants of conquered New France fought duels somewhat regularly. They occurred mostly between soldiers—and mostly between English ones. It is only in the 1830s that the French remembered duelling as a quick and fairly easy way to solve problems. These later duels were mostly caused by the tensions between French radicals and English Loyalists, perhaps a remnant of the constant English and French fighting overseas. There are records that French Canadians also exported their duelling habits elsewhere, namely to Louisiana, Illinois and the island of Martinique, among others, where the outcomes seemed to have been generally negative for the French fighters—they either ended up dead or scarred for life.

CHAPTER THREE

PAUL CHOMEDEY DE MAISONNEUVE AND FRENCH CANADIAN CATHOLICISM

By the time Paul Chomedey de Maisonneuve arrived, the French had created Canada and were mildly successful in using its resources and settling its territory. It was a rough time for French Canadians, and one thing that helped them get through the difficult winter months and other recurrent problems was religion, Roman Catholicism to be precise. Until the Quiet Revolution in Québec in the 1960s, the French Catholic Church was a powerful institution in the province, a power that goes back to the 1600s, when religion was something mysterious and fascinating. Religion provided solace for people living in hardship, some kind of hope that there was more to life than simply tilling the land, eating and sleeping. Maybe this was even more true for the French settlers who moved to an unknown land and survived harsh winters, rudimentary diets and homesickness.

The Catholic religion, with its promise of heaven, was very popular in early Canada. And, of course, the importance of the institution was soon recognized by means of a grant of land (30 percent of the Montréal colony's territory at one point) and also the grant of power. Experiencing a slow start, the Church eventually grew to be a powerful institution in the New World, ruling not only the spiritual lives of its followers, but also their personal lives. The Church had eyes everywhere; as soon as a small community formed, settlers automatically built a parish church. The parish priests were part of the community, advising people on everything from child-raising methods to management of their possessions to marriage duties. And some of the priests were definitely more insistent and zealous than others. For example, because procreation was so important for the survival of the colony, priests would often enquire about pregnancies in the settlement or the need for more "exercises" to enable them. (I need not be more specific.)

The French settlers brought Catholicism to Canada, and it remained an important part of the lives of French Canadians until fairly recently. Today, remnants of this religious influence linger, albeit in a rather unconventional way—French Canadians swear in Catholic. Indeed, our swear words are all religious terms: *baptême* (baptism), *calice* (chalice) and *tabernacle* are all terms used passionately by any French Canadian who smashes a finger with a hammer. While this might seem blasphemous, it is in fact a concrete example of the religious foundations of the French Canadians. When something happens suddenly or hurtfully enough to make you swear, and the first thing to slip out of your mouth is a term also used in religious ceremonies, it says something about the extent to which the Catholic religion has infiltrated the daily lives of French Canadians. Montréal cinematographer Louise Lamarre once said, "When you get mad, you look for words that attack what represses you." According to her, American swear words are usually sexual because of the Puritan origins of the country and their repression of sex. In Québec, it seems that when we swear, we are actually responding to centuries of repression by the Church. It does make sense that we would curse at something that controlled virtually every aspect of past generations' lives.

On a more serious note, the churches still standing today are a testimony to the French Catholic religion. In 1675, Sister Marguerite

Bourgeoys founded a church that she named after a wooden statue of Notre-Dame du Bon Secours she had brought with her from France. The small chapel was rebuilt after a fire, and the 1771 reconstructed version still stands in the Old Port of Montréal. Bourgeoys was, among other things, a chaperon for the *filles du roi*, of which we will learn a bit about later. The Notre-Dame du Bon Secours chapel now hosts the Marguerite-Bourgeoys Museum, which offers guided tours and educational visits. Montréal's most precious church is undoubtedly the Notre-Dame Basilica. This religious establishment was built in 1672 by the Sulpiciens, a denomination that, at one point, owned the entire island of Montréal. Because of the significant growth in population, the basilica was expanded twice. This French Catholic church is truly an institution in the city, and it occupies a central location in a popular tourist area. John Paul II visited the basilica in 1984, and it hosted Celine Dion's wedding and the funerals of both Maurice Richard and Pierre-Elliott Trudeau.

The St. Boniface Cathedral in Manitoba is another great institution. Initially a small chapel in the early 19th century, it grew to the size of a cathedral a couple of years later. Having survived two fires, it still stands today, rebuilt on the ruins of the previous building. The names of the bishops of this cathedral demonstrate the French influence in Manitoba: Monseigneurs Provencher, Taché, Langevin, Béliveau, Baudoux, Hacault and Goulet. Louis Riel, the well-known Métis and founder of Manitoba, is buried there, in the largest and oldest Catholic cemetery in the western provinces. The church of Sacré-Coeur in Saulnierville, Nova Scotia, is also a great piece of French architectural work. Built in the 1880s, it still stands today, a proud institution in the centuries-old fishing village. The very name of the town, Saulnierville (established in 1785) pays tribute to the Saulnier families who contributed to creating this community. The wood to build the church was all donated, and the residents of the parish contributed 25 days a year of volunteer work to help finish the project. French Canadians might swear in Catholic, but they do care about their churches.

Back in 17th-century France, the beginning of the Compagnie de Jésus, the Jesuits, along with other reforms, made religion more accessible to people. And because people can't simply adopt a new religion but they also feel compelled to tell other people to do the same, the Jesuits came to New France. The motivation to "spread the good news" was more powerful than ever, and what better place than Canada to bring the concepts found in the Catholic religion? The Natives obviously had a different belief system; French priests saw them as a huge population of heathens that needed to be converted. Heaven was only open to those who were baptized, so Jesuit priests thought it was their responsibility to make sure everyone got in. Maybe they were an early version of ticket scalpers, making sure everyone got a ticket, even though the price was sometimes high. In fact, for the longest time, the Natives thought the priests were responsible for the deaths of their loved ones because the Jesuits mostly baptized the dying. The newly baptized often passed away shortly after being touched by the priests, so it wasn't the best way to "sell" the religion.

The growing religious movement was responsible for the foundation of Ville-Marie (Montréal) in 1642. Ville-Marie, formerly called Hochelaga, was another Native village "found" by the Europeans and renamed. Paul Chomedey de Maisonneuve, a Frenchman from Champagne and a talented lute player, was the official founder of the new city. He continued Cartier's tradition by setting up a cross on the mountain to baptize the city, a colony that he hoped would be a self-sustaining, religious community. Ville-Marie became Montréal in 1763, a name based on the name of the mountain (Mont Réal) that overlooks the city.

Fairly recently, information was widely circulated about the mountain, stating that it was, in fact, a volcano. Geologists were asked to verify the information and determined that it was indeed a volcano that had been extinct for at least 125 million years. Nevertheless, the information was printed up in countless travel guides, making Montréal a tad less inviting to tourists.

In 1924, a new cross was constructed on top of the mountain/prehistoric volcano to commemorate Maisonneuve's gesture. A bit bigger than the original one, this one stands 30 metres tall and about nine metres wide and is made out of metal. A campaign to raise funds for the project was conducted, and it is thanks to 85,000 school children and their work that we are able today to see the cross from pretty much everywhere in Montréal. The founding of Ville-Marie/Montréal was motivated by religious fervour—the city was supposed to be a mystical colony dedicated to the Virgin Mary, with the hope that it would become a centre for religious conversion of the Natives. It is said that Maisonneuve had an epiphany when resting at home in France, as he was trying to keep informed of the goings on in society. He had heard of the British *Mayflower* expedition en route to establishing an American Protestant community and thought France should do the same. So France explored the world because others did; it sent people to colonize an overseas territory also because others had done so; and it founded a religious colony because if others could do it, then France could, too. It seems that many of France's accomplishments in the New World were based on jealousy and showboating. Either way, it did get things done.

As Maisonneuve and his team landed on the shore of the settlement would become Ville-Marie and knelt in devotion, the priest who accompanied Maisonneuve said:

> You are a grain of mustard-seed that shall rise and grow until its branches overshadow the land. You are few, but your work is the work of God. His smile is on you, and your children shall fill the land.

Maisonneuve and his companions began briskly setting up tents and fires, and a short three months after their arrival, they were proud to report the first baptism, that of a four-year-old Native child. In 1676, swearing was punishable by whipping, while in 1688, it became illegal to work on Sundays. Although the Catholic religion was an important part of the colonists' lives (it was important to get blessings for the home, for renovation projects, for livestock, and even for the wedding bed), its physical representation in the Church and its main representatives, the priests, were not as revered and were even sometimes disobeyed.

This trait was associated with the French Canadians, along with insubordination (because of the free lives of the *coureurs des bois*), an independent spirit (for people who lived away from their government for weeks on end) and the famous French *joie de vivre*.

But why did French men and women decide to leave their lives in France, undertake a usually dreadful overseas voyage and settle in an unknown land? For starters, the French had to live within a rigid social structure. What this meant was that there was no interclass mobility. If you were born poor, you would die poor. For tenants of a tiny parcel of land in France, the idea of being able to get a huge tract of land elsewhere was enough motivation to move pretty much anywhere, under whatever conditions. For middle-class individuals longing for noble status, it was the prospect of being awarded the title of *seigneur* once established in Canada that clinched the deal. Going from so-so status to a *seigneur* was a step up and, more importantly, this step was almost effortless, a good thing for nobles who were not used to working. Reaching another level in society was something they certainly would never be able to do in France. A good example of this breakdown of social barriers was the hunting of wild game, which was a privilege reserved for high nobility in France but open to everyone in Canada. For the most part, immigrants to Canada were soldiers, and they remained the most important group at least until the Conquest of 1760 (a deal struck by France and England in which the former gave all of New France to the latter). After that, they had no more territory to defend. For soldiers assigned to Canada, there was great incentive to remain in the country after their appointment was over since they automatically received a grant of land and a year's pay if they decided to stay. Otherwise, the bulk of the *habitant* population was made up of people of modest means who were promised a trip overseas and a piece of land they could call their own.

CHAPTER FOUR

THE SUN KING, LES FILLES DU ROI AND COLONIZATION

Despite some advantages, immigration was not really very popular. Fewer than 300 French men and women came to Canada between 1608 and 1640, and fewer than 1000 from then until 1660. There were so few people that a man condemned to death by Maisonneuve was able to get out of this small problem by accepting the job of executioner. No one could be found to execute criminals, which was probably a good thing in hindsight. A woman accused of murdering her husband had to be hanged in Québec City because there were no executioners in Montréal. The trip to Québec City must have been a really dreary one for this woman.

What didn't help the situation was that France also imposed restrictions on immigration. For example, prisoners and Protestants could not immigrate to New France, for the obvious reason that their presence was not welcome in the new territory. Prisoners would be too free in this land with no boundaries, and prisons were definitely not the first buildings constructed in a settlement. Protestants were not welcome in either France or New France because the French were still fuming about the new Church of England. France had come down hard on Protestants, who publicly questioned the sanctity of the Mass, and the Huguenots, as the Protestants were called in France, were persecuted throughout the kingdom. On an infamous day in 1572, French Catholics assassinated thousands of Huguenots in Paris. While estimates of the number of casualties differed from a couple of thousand to close to 100,000, the event confirmed the antipathy of the French population towards the Reformation and its consequences. It was understandable that the French did not want them in their newly peopled territory.

To add to this, the female population of French Canada was less than half that of its male counterpart (852 women in total came to New France), which slowed the growth of the population. Created by the king, the immigration program called *les filles du roi* worked towards bringing enough women for all the male settlers living in the colony. These "daughters of the king" came from orphanages or from farming communities, and they came to New France with the strict mission of finding a husband. There was, of course, a dowry awarded to them as soon as they got married—a great way to start common life. The dowry was highest if a woman married an officer, and it was also advantageous to tie the knot with a soldier. The necessity of finding someone to marry gave the impression that the women were "easy." Indeed, they needed to find someone fast, if only to be able to access their dowry money, which made them a bit more forward than women who had all the time they wanted to find a companion. It is evident that the first marriages were more business ventures than love—reproduction was the key to the colony's survival, and companionship was something that lonely settlers needed no matter what. Jack Verney, in his book on the Carignan-Salières regiment, agrees:

> The couple often had very little opportunity for meeting socially and privately before they were married. There were few public occasions to meet, except for the church, and social events, such as balls, were rarer still, the first ever being held in February 1667. After three or four

visits to the girl in her home, suitors were expected to start talking of their intentions to her parents, often with the parish priest keeping a watchful eye on the proceedings.

The king's idea worked, and some six or seven years after the first shipment of French women arrived, the colony recorded 700 births, and the male-to-female ratio was close to equal (there were six men for each woman in 1663). The farm girls were probably the best catch for a settler because they were strong and were used to hard and demanding work. If the new couple started a family early, there were great advantages. For example, families with 12 children or more were granted substantial monetary gifts. Having large families soon became a French Canadian tradition and remained so well into the 1950s. My parents' generation was probably one of the last to follow the practice; my father has five siblings and my mother had three brothers and a sister.

Another way to promote family life was to punish the men who decided to remain single by revoking their fur-trading permits or suspending their hunting privileges. Big families were also possible because girls would marry at about 12 or 13 years of age. As soon as they hit puberty, girls were expected to find a husband and begin a family, which offered several more pregnancy cycles than women living in France, where the average age of marriage was closer to 16 years old. The four more years or so of fertility that colonial women benefited from resulted in a sizeable contribution to population growth. Not only that, but it seemed the cold, fresh air of the New World was better on the women's constitutions than the heavy air of overpopulated France. The Canadian air made them less vulnerable to diseases, which spread faster in warm environments. Of course, deaths during labour and during the first two years of a child's life were common—there were no secret recipes to take away the risks borne by a mother and her children.

With less than 1000 relocated French citizens in 1660, how do we explain the survival of New France? By the sudden interest of King Louis XIV—nicknamed the Sun King—in the new colony. Louis XIV brought a certain pride in being French to his people, and what better way to prove this than to tell everyone who didn't want to hear it, namely, the Natives of Canada. He is remembered as the Great King, which by extension means the French experienced a "great" period in their history. When he took power, officially at five years of age, but technically only at 23, Louis XIV had already dealt with a small revolution (the Fronde) and had proven that he deserved the throne. Glory for his nation and for himself was probably what motivated him to promote settlement in his overseas colony. In fact, Louis XIV has often been studied in light of his achievements, because what was shown to the public differed greatly from what actually was. For example, we have no record of an older Louis, as paintings portrayed him as a young and vibrant king until his death.

Even though New France might have only been a flattering mirror for the king of France, the fact that he appreciated the status it gave him was good for the fledgling colony. One of the most important changes witnessed in that period was the promotion of immigration, and the associated development of the seignieurial régime. This régime was imported from France as a system for granting land to colonists. While the system was slowly crumbling in France, it worked well in Canada, perhaps because the powers of the landlords were not as overbearing and the lives of the tenants a tad more bearable. The system in France was nothing more than regulated slavery, and the poor folk tilling the earth had no hope of bettering their lives in any possible way. The difference here was that the *seigneurs* needed people on their land and could not afford to treat them badly. In France, it was exactly the opposite; too many people meant the nobility could treat their tenants badly and get new ones whenever they wanted to. So in a way, the *seigneurs* of New France were forced to be nicer "bosses" than their overseas cousins—they really had no other choice.

Each parcel of land needed access to water, so land was divided into lengthwise rectangular strips, with one of the narrow ends along a river. This division system, while it allowed individuals to have huge tracts of land, was done in such a way that neighbours were not that far from each other, and that closeness helped to develop a sense of community. Once all the land along a river was allocated, the ends of the lots were closed off, a road was built and another row of lots (called a *rang*) was allocated. Each *rang* became a small community. Everyone knew one another, and they all contributed to *rang* life by helping to build a market, a small chapel and a school.

Schools, or *écoles de rang*, as they were called, were usually small rooms that accommodated maybe 10 to 15 children, all of different ages. The school teacher, called either *institutrice* or *maîtresse d'école*, taught, among other things, French and mathematics—subjects that were useful for work on the farm. Attendance was not mandatory, and as soon as the harvesting period started on the farm, more often than not, the boys were taken out of school to work the land and the girls to work around the house. The schools in rural areas of Québec evolved slowly, adding perhaps a wood stove as technological advancement. By the 1950s, there were still many rural schools, a majority of them without electricity or running water. Québec schools waited until the 1960s for a complete revamping; the government required schools to centralize (that is, merge) and also funded their modernization.

The social structure of the small *rang* communities was created partly by the location of the lots: people close to the water were deemed better off than the ones behind them, with no access to the river. Today, this division still exists: if you drive around in the *campagne* in Québec, some streets are still called *rang*. And access to water, although not necessary anymore, is still considered a prized location for wealthier people. I live on the West Island of Montréal where Lakeshore Road, a name that matches its geographical location, is a very expensive street to live on, even though we now have no real use for access to water. Although the seigneurial system was abolished in 1854, the settlers (*habitants*) who wanted to stay on their land had to pay the *seigneurs* back for the land. Because of the high value of some of these parcels, it was decided that the settlers and their descendants would continue paying off their land to the *seigneurs* and their descendants until the full value had been repaid. It was only in 1945 that the Québec government decided that municipalities should wipe out the debts and move on. This means that a system installed in the early 17th century disappeared in the mid-20th century, just over 60 years ago.

CHAPTER FIVE

EXPANSION, COUREURS DES BOIS AND CULTURAL FRENCH CANADA

E xpansion within the territory soon became necessary in order to seek if not a sea route to China, at least a way to cross the North American continent completely. Expansion led to the popularization of the *coureur des bois* profession (in English, literally "runners of the woods"), men who would get their furs directly from the Natives instead of waiting for them to show up at a trading post. They could get better deals by visiting the villages, all the while establishing positive contact with most of them, something that had not necessarily happened previously. The *coureurs* developed closer and more personal relationships with the Natives, which made them more inclined to absorb the Native culture and perhaps to understand their side of things. The *coureurs* were not really accepted by the governing authorities because they did not help in the colonization effort and lived in unregulated areas with the liberty to make their fortunes as they saw fit. Complete liberty was not something Frenchmen were used to, and they thoroughly enjoyed it. They disappeared for months, sometimes years, and took on the Native way of life, which, of course, was considered to be a life of sacrilege, at least according to the Church.

The *coureurs'* long absences and the lack of news from them gave birth to the myth of the *chasse-galerie*, a precious piece of Québec folklore. According to the legend, the spirits of the *coureurs des bois* (whether they were dead or simply gone for a long time) would appear on New Year's Eve in a flying canoe that was said to be propelled by Satan. Originally, the *chasse-galerie* was a French legend that told the story of a man who liked hunting so much that he would skip Mass to run after wild animals. For his punishment, he had to fly in the sky for eternity, chased by the animals he was trying to kill. Once the French came to the New World, the legend became mixed up with some Native stories that added the flying canoe part. The story was popularized by journalist Honoré Beaugrand, an accomplishment that has earned him a metro line bearing his name in Montréal. Here is the final paragraph of the legend by Beaugrand, where he "recollects" his night spent in the flying canoe:

> All that I can say my friend is that it is not as funny as we think to go see your girlfriend in a canoe, in the middle of winter, while running the *chasse-galerie*; even less so if you have a drunkard as the driver. If you believe me, you will wait next summer to go kiss your sweet love, instead of taking the risk to travel with the devil.

The story made sense when palced in a context in which the priests frowned upon the lifestyle of the *coureurs* and that damnation was what they had to look forward to for not observing the religious rites. It also illustrated in a way how the Canadian winter had remained somewhat enveloped in mystery. Since the beginning of exploration, the snowy season brought a screeching halt to any type of outdoor activity. Missing your departure in the summer meant you had to stay in the colony until late spring the following year. It also meant not being able to grow food, no easy access to water and cold, plain old freezing Canadian cold. Today, cold weather is kind of a Canadian trademark and a source of pride—

only real Canadians can survive a real winter. But back then, winter must have been a scary season.

Escaping from the rigid rules imposed by the Church and the government, the *coureurs des bois* rarely wanted to be part of society—they felt uncomfortable being in town, and winter was not the only reason why they left for long periods. Even though their work contributed to the economy, the *coureurs* had a pretty bad reputation, as expressed in this quotation by author Brigitte Purkhardt in her book *La Chasse-galerie*:

> The life of the *coureur des bois* is a perpetual idleness which leads them to debauchery of all kinds. They sleep, they smoke, they drink *eau-de-vie* no matter what it costs, and they debauch the women and the girls of the Natives. They live in entire independence, they don't owe anything to anyone, they recognize no superior, no judge, no law, no police and no subordination.

This interest in a nomadic existence could have been influenced by the Natives, but it was taken on freely by New France men, who made it their own, transforming it into the *joie de vivre*, the enjoyment for life that we associate with French Canadians today. By the 1680s, the French government wanted to regulate this little problem and started issuing permits for the *coureurs des bois*, which gave way to a new generation of *coureurs*, the *voyageurs*, whose only difference from their predecessors was that they were "legal." Probably the best-known *coureur des bois* was Pierre-Esprit Radisson, born around 1636 in Paris, who was instrumental in establishing the Hudson's Bay Company, alongside his brother-in-law, Médard Chouart Desgroseillers. Radisson came to live in Trois-Rivières and was adopted by the Iroquois after he was caught roaming around alone. This proof of his courage (or temerity, depending on how you look at it) impressed the Iroquois enough that they invited him to come and live with them. Not all of the tribe agreed with this decision, and paint they put on Radisson's face and body expressed their ambivalence—he was painted half white and half black, meaning that he might be accepted by the tribe or he could be killed. He survived this episode in the New World and ended up living the good life in London until his death in 1710. Radisson went from being a member of a Native tribe to being an English gentleman.

Radisson was French but was only true to his two passions: exploration and fur trading. He organized an expedition to Lake Superior in 1668, something no one had done before, and he found enough furs there to fill

100 canoes, or so it is said. But the expedition had no permit (a capital sin at the time), so he was fined upon his return and the furs were confiscated. In retaliation, he changed sides and joined the British (who wouldn't have in his situation). He and his brother-in-law apparently lied their way to getting an expedition paid for by the English, telling tales of furs flowing from everywhere, of animals that didn't even exist and of Natives who looked very strange. Radisson was not a faithful Frenchman, but he did make an important contribution to his homeland, establishing trading posts farther inland, and thus opening up more territory for exploration. But most importantly, in 1670, he and his brother-in-law convinced the English government to grant a charter for fur trading to a company called The Governor and Company of Adventurers of England Trading into Hudson's Bay (later known as the Hudson's Bay Company) that would greatly influence the development of Canada.

The *coureur des bois* ideal lived on long after the passing of Radisson and his fictional stories in the form of the French Canadian lumberjacks, the *bucherons*, who also travelled deep into the woods and earned good pay, cutting the wood instead of living in it. The image of the lumberjack has come to represent French Canadians in the eyes of anyone outside the country who learns about us. The French Canadian is always pictured as a bearded man wearing a red and black plaid shirt. The lumberjacks, because they took work wherever they could, contributed to the spread of the French Canadian population. The timber industry in Québec still employs about 150,000 French Canadians, while its exports are worth close to $12 million annually. Nationwide, the industry has been making news over the softwood lumber issue with the United States. The wave of discontent in Canada means that this is still an important industry. Nevertheless, the lumberjacks of today do not necessarily wear plaid shirts, although most tourists to Québec are disappointed when they realize this.

The log drive (*drave*) was one of the sub-industries crucial to French Canadian employment, especially in the Mauricie region of Québec. The St. Maurice River was used until 1995 to carry huge logs downstream from the woods where they were cut to pulp-and-paper mills situated right on the banks of the river. The *bucherons* then left home for the northern woods as soon as winter was over and returned only when the first snow fell. While they were absent only half as long as the *voyageurs*, they were still considered nomads in the light of the slow urbanization of Québec and the urgent need for people to go elsewhere to find work.

For a while, however, the French Canadians' tendency to move around for work, either in the woods or in the mines throughout the nation, demonstrated that perhaps opportunities were scarce for them. One hit TV series in Québec, *Les Filles de Caleb*, inspired by a novel by Arlette Cousture, illustrated just that. It followed the lives of a school teacher and a lumberjack who was forced to leave his home regularly for long periods, although in this romanticized version of the *coureur de bois* life, his travels were motivated by deep feelings rather than a lack of money.

CHAPTER SIX

CONQUEST, CONFEDERATION AND BEYOND

New France had an obligation to take part in any conflict that France entered into. A similar understanding existed in the south, which meant that when the two countries, Britain and France, went to war, their overseas colonies were also fighting. Conflict began with the Seven Years' War in 1756, the first worldwide conflict, since prior to that, the wars had only been continent-wide. Because of their relatively low importance on the chessboard, the colonies were usually, at the time of end-of-war treaties, pocket change for European nations and were often exchanged to even out a deal. After a complete turnaround in the power alliances of Europe, Britain, allied with Prussia, declared war on France, now allied with a former adversary, Austria—a true soap-opera switch of allegiance (hard to follow, but yet so entertaining). In the Americas, the conflict began in 1754 when an American general, a certain George Washington, ambushed a French unit in Ohio. In a fight against the American colonies, New France seemed doomed—while the American territory counted more than 1.4 million people, the French colonies recorded a mere 62,500 souls.

Despite this, the Canadian way of fighting resulted in some victories for the colony—the soldiers stopped an American advance near Lake Champlain and captured the forts in the Great Lakes and Lake George regions. The "Canadian" way of fighting was borrowed from the Natives. Back then, the British (and most Europeans) fought in formations, that is, they would group together in straight lines and advance towards an enemy. While it must have been really pretty to see, the strategy wasn't very effective; the two fighting groups would march towards each other while firing and hope for the best. The Canadians had learned a new fighting method from their Native neighbours—hiding and ambushing their opponents. It took a while for people to realize that surprising an enemy as more effective than walking in a straight line right in front of them. So the French Canadians hid, then ambushed and scared the heck out of the British, at least a few times. In 1759, however, the loss of Fort Niagara and the advance of 9000 British soldiers to Québec City ended with the defeat of the French. After a three-month siege, the decisive battle of the Plains of Abraham lasted only an hour and signed the death warrant of New France. The Plains of Abraham, now a public park, is protected by the National Battlefields Commission. Redesigned in 1908, it was the first officially designated historic site in Canada and a gift from the Canadian government in honour of Québec City's tercentenary celebrations. It is where the city's largest events, festivals and get-togethers take place. It is also the place where St. Jean Baptiste celebrations are the most elaborate. Although the Plains of Abraham should be remembered as a site of defeat, Quebeckers have decided to focus instead on the importance of the French in their history.

After the defeat on the Plains of Abraham, New France consisted of Montréal and Trois-Rivières, both of which eventually capitulated after a dreadful siege. Interestingly, the last battle of the Seven Years' War on Canadian soil was won by the French in Sainte-Foy, although it made no significant difference after the fiasco on the Plains. The British had managed to stop French ships that were bringing reinforcements to help the colony, so the

French Canadians had to fight alone. New France was gone, conquered by the British. During the dealings between the two nations, France could have ask for New France back, but the French government chose instead the colonies of Martinique and Guadeloupe. Even though this seems harsh, it was a sound business decision—the two islands were important sugar-producing territories, while New France only had furs to offer. And since the importance of fur was dependent on fashion, it was a pretty volatile product. Plus, if one was to choose a place for its weather and landscape, perhaps Guadeloupe was a more logical choice. In the cold months of winter, I would choose it in a second.

So the Conquest happened, and New France was officially handed over to the British in 1763 by means of the Treaty of Paris. As winter set in, both sides prepared for the cold period. Nothing really changed; people simply learned to coexist during these few months. The colonies were in shambles because nobody had thought of planting, growing and harvesting food between two bloody battles. To make things worse, there were twice as many people in the small villages as there were before because British soldiers had remained on site to keep the peace. At the beginning of winter, some British soldiers were nice enough to either give or sell some of their rations to starving

French Canadians, but soon everyone was in the same boat (actually, in the same snowbank would be a more appropriate expression). It is tempting to say that after the Conquest, the French and the English hated each other, but it seems that our awful winter actually helped iron out their differences, at least for a while.

The situation remained the same for a bit, that is, until 1774. Trouble was brewing in the American colonies, because the colonists had grown tired of having a foreign power making decisions for them. The Americans were talking of independence, a pretty scary thought for the British, whose flag, at this point, was flying in half the countries of the world. Because French Canadians were still the majority in what had been New France, the British government grew concerned that perhaps the French would join forces with the Americans and ask for independence as well. As a preemptive strike, the British passed the Québec Act of 1774, which, among other things, allowed the French Canadians to practice their religion and keep their legal system, at least for managing their private matters. The Québec Act also defined the boundaries of the Province of Québec, which was much larger than one would think. The area encompassed Québec, southern Ontario, Indiana, Illinois, Michigan, Ohio, Wisconsin and Minnesota. New France's name was thus changed to Québec, if only because it seemed weird to have New France as the property of Old England. The Québec Act was effective, and as a result, the French Canadians refused to help the Americans, even when they came to Québec to try to convince them. So the Québec Act and the refusal of the French to support the American rebellion probably kept Canada from becoming part of the United States. Although French Canadians are sometimes seen as wanting to divide the country, they were the first to consciously save it from the Americans.

After the American Revolution, the language makeup of the region changed quite a bit. British Americans who had remained faithful to Britain had to escape the United States because they were now considered traitors to the new country. While some of them moved back to England, most of them were more practical and simply crossed the border into New France, a British-held territory. These new residents, British Loyalists as they were called, congregated in what is now Ontario, and they became as numerous as the French Canadians. Soon, the newly arrived English realized they needed a different form of government because what was there had been instituted with the French Canadians in mind and their status as a conquered people. After the Loyalists petitioned the British government, the Constitutional Act of 1791 came into effect, creating two provinces: Lower Canada (present-day Québec) and Upper Canada (roughly what is now Ontario). Lower Canada was predominantly French speaking and Catholic, and Upper Canada was comprised of Protestant British Loyalists. The act also enabled each province to form its own legislative assembly, although these political entities did not have much power.

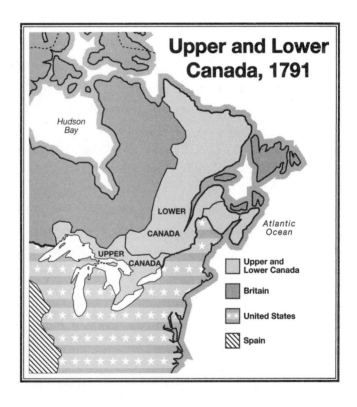

The English-speaking population slowly grew larger and larger and gained more and more power, both political and economic. The situation was the result of an increase in the number of English Canadians, but there was something else. It seem that for a while, French Canadians did not really care about participating in this new political "arrangement," which seemed to isolate them even more. Eventually, French Canadians realized that they should be allowed rights and be better represented in government. They also wished to speak their own language, whether at home or in their legislative assembly.

In 1834, a group of French Canadian politicians introduced a bill called the 92 Resolutions (which we will speak more of in Chapter 9), consisting of a number of requests concerning language, representation and economic issues. When each and every one of the resolutions was refused, trouble began brewing in Lower Canada. Disgruntled men, who called themselves the *Patriotes*, gathered in the countryside and launched an attack, which was soon stopped by British soldiers. The city of St. Eustache, one of the towns where the *Patriotes* were beaten back, became a symbol of the rebellion. After defeating the rebellious French Canadians, the British pillaged the area to send a message. While we think of the 1837–38 rebellions as French Canadian discontent gone wrong, we often forget that there was also a rebellion in Upper Canada.

When news arrived there that the *Patriotes* were rebelling, armed attacks were organized by a man named William Lyon Mackenzie, the grandfather of one of our prime ministers. These attacks were as unsuccessful as the rebellions in Lower Canada, and soon the *Patriotes* were arrested, put on trial and some were hanged. There is a monument dedicated to the *Patriotes* in Montréal, right in front of the prison in which they were held during their trial.

Even if the rebellions were not successful (to say the least), they led to something—the Act of Union of 1841. This act was a direct response to a report on the rebellions written by Lord Durham, which called for the union of Lower and Upper Canada into the Province of Canada. The territory known as Lower Canada was renamed Canada East, and Upper Canada became Canada West. If this was intended to prevent confusion with the previous names, that idea failed miserably. Indeed, a question about the former names of Ontario and Québec was always a trick question on history exams when I was young. Durham thought that by uniting the two provinces, the French would eventually become assimilated, and the "Francophone problem" would simply disappear. Brilliant. Soon, English immigration changed the population makeup in the favour of English Canadians. The united Parliament meant that English was the only official language, and that the French Canadians would be under-represented.

It was eventually suggested that the surrounding territories be brought together and a form of government in which every province would have equal rights and representation set up. The signing of the 1867 constitution, however, included only Ontario, Québec, New Brunswick and Nova Scotia. This first constitution was ratified in Québec City, host of the second conference of the Dominion negotiations.

One of the Fathers of Confederation, Georges-Étienne Cartier, was a French Canadian who

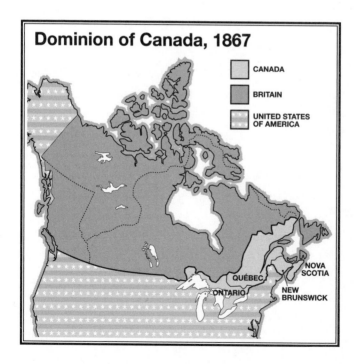

Dominion of Canada, 1867

CANADA
BRITAIN
UNITED STATES OF AMERICA

QUÉBEC
ONTARIO
NOVA SCOTIA
NEW BRUNSWICK

had fought in the *Patriotes* rebellion but ended up co-premier of the united Canadas along with John A. Macdonald. He had to hide for several years because of his participation in the rebellion, and he must have been good at it because rumours of his death started circulating during his time in exile. The fact that he was able to make the British government forget about this little blip in his life is amazing; he must have been quite a smooth talker. His wife would have probably agreed with this statement, seeing as he spent the last years of his life with her own cousin instead of her. Cartier had a pretty peculiar past. He came close to fighting two duels, avoiding one because his opponent signed an apology and the other because the police showed up before it started

Although we often equate French Canada with separation, Cartier, one of the foremost Fathers of Confederation was a proud Canadian. He was one of the most vocal proponents of a union between the Canadas and the Maritime provinces. Cartier also contributed to the purchase of the North West Territories and the political creation of the province of Manitoba, and he was instrumental in getting British Columbia to join the Confederation. What we consider to be, in effect, the physical creation of Canada, the construction of the Canadian Pacific Railway, was initially introduced by Cartier in the House of Commons.

Cartier was a French Canadian who helped create Canada politically. His belief in the advantages of Confederation was best illustrated in a poem he wrote about Canada, perhaps an inspiration for the anthem we later adopted:

> As the old proverb says:
> Nothing is more beautiful than one's country;
> And to sing it is the tradition;
> And mine I sing to my friends
> The stranger looks with an envious eye
> On the St. Lawrence, the majestic course;
> At its aspect the Canadian sings:
> O Canada! My country! My love!

As for the official anthem of the country, "O Canada," the words were also written by a Frenchman, a judge named Adolphe-Basile Routhier. The English words took a lot longer and went through several versions before a text was finally adopted in 1908. The song officially became our anthem in 1980, replacing the still-standing, completely anachronistic "God Save the Queen." The music for our anthem was composed by Calixa Lavallée, the direct descendent of a soldier in the Carignan-Salières regiment. The glorious hymn was first sung in 1880 on a particular date: June 24. This day is now a holiday in Québec, celebrating St. Jean Baptiste. It is primarily a Francophone celebration, and those who organize some of the events are often thought to be associated with separatism. Lavallée had a brilliant career in the U.S., but while he lived in Canada, his talent was not recognized as much. He publicly declared being in favour of the annexation of Canada to its southern neighbour, which might have been a reason for his unpopularity here and immense popularity down south.

French Canadians are proud to be Canadian. Whenever one of our athletes wins a gold medal in the Olympics, we hear one of the most poignant French legacies. In addition, a French Canadian, Jacques St. Cyr, designed the maple leaf in our Canadian flag, while the idea of the maple leaf was suggested by Eugene Fiset, a distinguished soldier. The flag was first hoisted in 1965, and its design was motivated by the upcoming centenary of the Confederation. While it is usually underlined that the flag was the work not of a single person but of a series of collaborators, it is befitting in this book to demonstrate how the French have contributed to our national symbols.

CHAPTER SEVEN

BILINGUAL CANADA

The most important influence of the French in Canada is that their language has remained one of our official languages. Latin in its roots, French is always evolving and was officially recognized as France's language in 1539. I remember a song we had to learn in primary school that described the beauty of the French language. I have included a few of the verses, testament to the most important legacy of Cartier, Champlain and others. I have attempted to translate these verses to the best of my knowledge. Trust me, it sounds much better in French than in my translation:

Elle a jeté des ponts par-dessus
l'Atlantique
Elle a quitté son nid pour un autre terroir
Et comme une hirondelle au printemps
des musiques
Elle revient nous chanter ses peines et
ses espoirs

Nous dire que là-bas dans ce pays de
neige
Elle a fait face aux vents qui soufflent
de partout,
Pour imposer ses mots jusque dans les
collèges
Et qu'on y parle encore la langue de chez
nous.

English translation:

It built bridges over the Atlantic
It left its nest for another territory
And as a swallow in the spring of music
It comes back to sing its woes and hopes

Over there in a country of snow
It fought the winds coming from
everywhere
To impose its words all the way into
colleges
And now the language from home is
still spoken there.

No matter how beautiful it may be, French is a difficult language to learn, with its many rules and as many exceptions, which explains why Canadians who don't learn it in their youth will often choose not to learn it at all. Although they are technically the same language, Québec French and "French" French are quite different. I spent some time on the French island of Martinique, and I had trouble being understood because of my accent. French Canadians have, of course, altered many words and have also adopted new ones. A *dépanneur* in Québec is a corner store, but it is a tow truck in France. We have also "francicized" many English words, which simply means using English words but pronouncing them with a French accent, like "babysitting," "living room" and "marketing."

In Ontario, I was surprised to hear most people rolling their *r*'s, which seems to be part of everyone's accent, at least in Sudbury. My in-laws once played an old audiotape of my husband and his sister when they were really young, and their accent sounded very strange to me, all the more because they have since lost it. Their use of *Pépére* as a nickname for their grandfather was funny to me only because it sounded more like *Pépérrrrre*. Nevertheless, my kids now use this appellation, probably because we often repeated it, in a joking manner. In any case, the French language is probably one of the only links between the many French communities, considering how differently their histories, and thus their identities, have developed. It is also comforting to know that if you are French, you can travel across Canada and hear the language, whether in a community or in a government office.

If we compare the French language within Canada to the French across Europe, however, our version of the language is a bit more standardized than it is across the Atlantic. The accent of the Maritimers is peculiar, incorporating a significant number of English words. In fact, a sentence in Chiac, the dialect in Nova Scotia, will usually have as many French words as English ones. Small differences are noticeable throughout Canada, of course, which are only obvious to other French people. I am thus unable to tell you what accent the French in Montréal have, since this is the norm for me and the standard by which I compare the accent in other regions. I do notice differences elsewhere, which does not mean that their pronunciation is better or worse than in Montréal.

Several words remain from our French ancestors, and those can be traced back to specific regions of France. For example, the use of the word *barrer* (to lock) comes from Normandy, while *boucherie* (butcher shop) comes from Poitou. Some words come to us from the

Natives, such as *boucane* (smoke from a fire), *atoca* (cranberry purée) and *ouaouaron* (bullfrog). If you use these words in France, they will have absolutely no idea what you are talking about. The argument has been made that our accent here in Québec can be traced back to the way French settlers spoke when they immigrated to Canada, that is, Old French. Indeed, our alteration of certain words seems not to have occurred here but was instead imported from 17th-century France. This would make the French Canadian language the original French language, though I'm not sure that all French people would agree.

The French language we speak is related to the Latin language spoken during the time of the Roman Empire. The earliest document written in French, "*Les Serments de Strasbourg*" (The Oaths of Strasbourg) dates back to 842 CE; it was a pledge of allegiance between Frankish kings. Years and years of evolution have changed the language quite a bit, to the point where it is now incomprehensible to us. The Middle Ages saw the Roman language divided into two: Latin, which was used by the Church and its representatives, and vernacular French, which was the common language used by everyone, including literary artists. In fact, vernacular French was declared the official language of France in 1539 thanks to Francis I, the king who also pushed for worldwide exploration. Many dialects developed throughout the kingdom, and in the 17th century, the Académie française was created to "purify" the language, so to speak. Whatever developments occurred in France, most probably became the norm in Canada soon afterwards. But like every other language, the French in Canada took on words and accents from our neighbours, whether they were English, Scottish or Native. French is an official language in 28 other countries besides Canada and is spoken by some 72 million people. And despite having lost out to English in terms of worldwide utilization in business and culture, French remains the second most studied language in the world. So Canadians who know both official languages have knowledge of two tremendously influential languages and cultures. As a completely unbiased observer, I think that Canadians are well equipped to take over the world...one hockey game at a time.

So Canada is bilingual, the most obvious demonstration of the influence of the French in the country's making. How did this happen? Is our country really bilingual everywhere? Let's try to summarize the history of bilingualism in Canada. New France was a French bastion in America, and it remained that way until the French were conquered by the British. The first inhabitants of every province and territory were French, and so the first European language spoken everywhere in our country was French. With the arrival of the British, the language makeup changed, but what really modified the proportion of French to English was not the Conquest of 1760. Rather, it was the American Revolution. Yes, I know, the Americans stick their noses into absolutely everything. The revolution in the south was a determining factor in bringing waves and waves of English-speaking immigrants north, who most often chose Ontario or the Maritimes as their new home.

These immigrants were known as the United Empire Loyalists, Americans who were against the Revolution and remained loyal to Britain (that is, they were on the losing side of the conflict). Between 40 and 50,000 Loyalists came to Canada either before the uprising, after having fought for the British or after their estates and everything they owned had been taken away. This important influx of English-speaking people gave birth in 1791 to Upper Canada (Ontario). The creation of Upper and Lower Canada was part of a plan to establish a representative government for the colony.

Outnumbered at first by the people in Lower Canada (formerly New France), the English-speaking population grew rapidly and expanded into the western part of the country, eventually by means of the developing railway system. A couple of generations later, the English-speaking population outnumbered the French Canadians. The government was British, so Loyalists were welcomed with open arms. Let's face it, the fact that they fought against the rebellious Americans to keep the whole continent British made them look pretty good. They also rapidly gained political control, and their language predominated in government dealings.

It is this switch that concerned the French population; perhaps more had to be done for the sake of their language and culture. The Québec Act of 1774, which allowed the French to practice their religion and speak their language, was not enough anymore, since English was spoken everywhere the French went. The minority position the French Canadians occupied in government affairs was striking. Some historians have argued that it was because of a lack of interest on the part of the French. Indeed, it is true that up until the World War I, the French population was living as if on a reserve. Their growing discontent would eventually find a voice and start a rebellion that didn't really succeed, the *Patriote* rebellions of 1837–38, which will be discussed in greater detail later on. Suffice it to say here that what the *Patriote*s were fighting for was, essentially, to have more power in government.

Lord Durham, a governor assigned to report on the causes of the rebellion, recommended the union of the two Canadas in order to assimilate the French, who according to him, apparently had no history. This report may have been a "wake-up call" for French Canada, a push to demonstrate that, to the contrary, French Canada had a rich history and rights that went with it; if they didn't, then I wouldn't have much to write about, right? The Act of Union was passed in 1841 and created the province of Canada. The act was unfair for Lower Canada (New France), which was treated as a minority while being forced to absorb the larger debt of Upper Canada. This act also forbade the use of the French language in official functions. With the joint effort of reformers Louis Hyppolite Lafontaine and Robert Baldwin (members of the Reform Party), the Act of Union was modified in order to make it more palatable for Lower Canada.

The collaboration between Lafontaine and Baldwin was brought to life in one of the "Heritage Minutes" commercials on CBC, where Lafontaine goes to Toronto to get elected, becoming the first French Canadian elected in Ontario. That commercial failed to show an important trait of Lafontaine's, if we trust the words of people who saw him in person—apparently, Lafontaine looked so much like Napoleon Bonaparte that when he visited Paris in the 1850s, people got excited. Not to say that his appearance did not elicit any reaction in

Canada, but looking like Napoleon must have been a showstopper, no doubt about it.

Lafontaine made Canadian politics exciting, if only because one of the bills he introduced caused a riot. Lafontaine's Rebellion Losses bill, which ordered the government to pay compensation to Lower Canadians whose property had been damaged during the rebellion, got people in Montréal really angry, mostly the Anglophone commercial class. Apparently, a similar bill had been presented in Upper Canada, but the people there thought it was a good idea. In Montréal, however, the bill was seen as giving too much power to Québec and was so badly received that a group of people stormed into Lafontaine's house and broke his furniture, ripped his window coverings and set fire to his stable. They also threatened to assassinate him and assaulted him several times as he walked down the street. Anyone who says that Canadian politics is boring is completely wrong. Lafontaine made politics a kind of a calling, at least for a while. Nowadays, the only thing our politicians have to fear is getting a cream pie in the face—not very life-threatening...unless you are violently lactose intolerant.

Besides making politics interesting, Lafontaine worked tremendously hard for the French Canadians, first and foremost by abolishing the land tenure system, one of the demands at the heart of the rebellion. This change was a huge one, because it changed the whole structure of Québec society. It is hard to believe that an agricultural system implemented in the 17th century was still in use more than 200 years later. Most importantly, Lafontaine demonstrated that it was possible to keep the French culture alive by working hard towards reforming what didn't work. Instead of rebelling or rejecting the existing system, he suggested a new option—participating in government and trying to change things in a more effective way.

Confederation, although it meant getting together with a bunch of English-speaking territories, also meant that signing up would be an opportunity to negotiate a better deal for the French population. Since each province had its own demands that it wanted fulfilled before joining Confederation, it was only natural that Québec made some requests as well. The most important of these came in the negotiation for optional bilingualism, which became section 133 of the British North America Act of 1867 (also called the BNA Act or the Constitution Act):

> Either the English or the French Language may be used by any Person in the Debates of the Houses of the Parliament of Canada and of the Houses of the Legislature of Québec; and both those

Languages shall be used in the respective Records and Journals of those Houses; and either of those Languages may be used by any Person or in any Pleading or Process in or issuing from any Court of Canada established under this Act, and in or from all or any of the Courts of Québec.

This was a pretty impressive achievement in terms of what had previously existed. What the above paragraph meant was that people were allowed to speak in Parliament in whichever language they wished, and since not everyone was bilingual, the government would provide interpreters to make sure that everyone understood one another (not that they would agree with each other). This also meant that documents issued from the legislatures, Parliament and other government institutions had to be published in both French and English. This optional bilingualism was only valid in government, however, and English remained the main language of the business world. Depending on how many people dozed off in parliamentary sessions, the number of people concerned with the new rule might have been pretty small. When compared to today's regulations on language, that article from the BNA Act doesn't seem like much. But back then, it was a great achievement, if only because it opened the door just enough to allow other language laws to be developed.

French was, in this way, acknowledged as an important language in Canada, enough that provisions had to be made for it in a founding document (the BNA Act). George-Étienne Cartier, and the other men who eventually signed the document, all contributed to making Canada a bilingual country. It would have been easy to dismiss the French and simply go on as an English-speaking nation, but they were numerous, and they had demonstrated, through the failed rebellion, that they were vocal and aware of their rights. Still today, politicians always have to make room for Québec's particular demands and areas of interests in order to obtain nationwide support. Québec is always a crucial place to visit for Canada's premiers or wannabe premiers. That is why our leaders always make an effort to speak French when they are in Québec—a nice courtesy, even though sometimes their accent makes the language a bit incomprehensible. But I guess it goes the other way, too, an example being Jean Chrétien's strong Henglish accent.

Besides bilingualism in government, another important step in the survival of French in Canada was education in their own language. The Church's stronghold on Québec's educational system meant that French education was not an issue. This was not the case in the rest of Canada. The Ontario government passed a bill (Regulation 17) in 1912 that dramatically reduced French-language education. The bill called for a more restricted use of French in the first years of education, and then...nothing. No French taught in schools at all. It has been suggested that this piece of legislation was a response to the refusal of the French Canadians to fight alongside the British in the Boer War in the 1890s.

In any case, Regulation 17 meant that the sizeable French population in Ontario could no longer be educated in their mother tongue and were not even allowed to learn the language in school. In Ottawa, the École Guigues has remained a symbol of the Franco-Ontarian fight for French education, especially in the context of the infamous Regulation 17. The school was closed after teachers refused to follow the new rule, but these dedicated educators kept teaching, hiding in other buildings. Considering how liberal Canada is perceived in today's world, the idea that Franco-Ontarian teachers had to hide with students to teach them to speak their mother tongue seems strange. These teachers found a way to occupy the closed school by using the pretext of daycare needs, and thanks to their tenacity, the school was eventually reopened.

The regulation was repealed in 1927, not only because of its blatant attack on human rights, but also because it became a bargaining chip in another negotiation between the premiers of Ontario and Québec. Rightfully or not, Howard Ferguson, the Ontario premier, went down in history as being responsible for the repeal...even if he didn't mean it. Actually, Ferguson is remembered for this and also for easing Prohibition laws—"Fergie's foam" was a 4.4-percent beer that appeared on the market following Ferguson's success in bringing beer back into our lives. So, Ferguson's legacy is French in schools and beer at home—I would have liked him, I'm sure.

It wasn't until 1968 that the Ontario government officially recognized French-language schools. My husband's grandfather, whom he lovingly calls "Mo," was proud to be a teacher in the first French-language high school in Ontario, the MacDonald Cartier school, opened in 1969 in Sudbury and still going strong in 2008. Fittingly, the name honours both John A. Macdonald and George-Étienne Cartier, two Fathers of Confederation, one French and one English, proof that when both groups work together, great things get done... like the creation of a country.

In the late 19th century, the problem of French education arose in western Canada, where English and French schools were seperated and publicly funded, which meant there was much less funding available for French schools. More people speaking English meant more money to educate them, and the opposite was true for the French. When the Act of Manitoba was adopted in 1870, the equality of the French language was provided for, but the act soon became outdated because there were streams of English-speaking immigrants taking over the territory. In 1890, the Schools Act abolished French as an official language in Manitoba and stopped the funding of French-language schools completely. The Northwest Territories followed suit a few years later.

In 1963, Lester B. Pearson established a Royal Commission on Bilingualism and Biculturalism whose mission was to assess the state of bilingualism in Canada and to determine ways to guarantee an equal partnership between the two cultures. The 1960s were in full swing, and Québec was beginning to show signs of discontent. There was a similar feeling in most of the French communities in the country. The Commission seemed to be a way to find out if we were still indeed bilingual. It was headed by André Laurendeau and Davidson Dunton, first chairman of the CBC. Laurendeau was considered one of the early nationalists, trying to get people to vote "no" in the plebiscite for conscription during World War II. Laurendeau was also a TV personality, hosting a weekly show called *Pays et Merveilles*.

The report that came out of the Commission, at a staggering cost I'm sure, was a "short" six-volume edition. It studied three major issues: bilingualism in government, the role of organizations in establishing good relations between the two "solitudes" and the extent to which people were able to become bilingual. If these were the three areas the Commission concentrated on, then they must have been the largest problems that existed at the time—no real bilingual government (although it was supposed to have been bilingual since Confederation), no attempts to bring Anglos and Francos together and no incentive for Anglophones to learn to speak French.

The conclusions of the report sparked a great wave of reforms, first and foremost the Official Languages Act, which was enacted in 1969. The report concluded that the French were under-represented in the Canadian government, that French schooling was deficient when compared to its English counterpart and that French was often a hindrance when trying to find employment. As a random example, many Canadian mining communities had the same social structure—French miners and English bosses. Most mining towns in northern Canada presented a clear separation between the workers, who lived close to the mine, and the supervisors, who lived in the suburbs. For members of the workers' communities, speaking only French was definitely not an asset, at least if one wanted to get ahead in a company.

Shortly after the publication of the report, the government announced its support for French education, and nine provinces quickly allowed the French language back into the education system. The Commission's report also enticed New Brunswick to declare itself officially bilingual, while Ontario at least improved its political attitude towards its French population. A decision by the Supreme Court ruled that the 1890 law that banned the use of French in Manitoba was illegal, and the language was restored as one of the province's official languages. The Commission was truly a turning point in the history of bilingualism, if only because it actually acknowledged that remaining bilingual required continuous work. This particular commission was effective, but we can't say the same for all the commissions that we fund as taxpayers. Reasonable accommodations, anyone?

Even though some of the recommendations of the 1963 commission were received negatively, it did help create a Ministry of Multiculturalism, now a Canadian Heritage program. The French are on the list of ethnic communities in Canada, although it is certainly a bit sad that the French have lost their place as the foremost ethnic group in Canada. Nevertheless, one should interpret the status of French Canadians in a positive light—being a recognized ethnic group means that the language, culture and rights of that community are respected, something French Canadians have been fighting for since...well, the Conquest. The mission statement of this new Canadian program on heritage talks about the bilingualism of the nation, among other things:

> We work together to promote culture, the arts, heritage, official languages, citizenship and participation, multiculturalism, Aboriginal, youth, and sport initiatives.

When the Official Languages Act was enacted in 1969, both French and English became official languages in federal institutions. In 1973, the adoption of a resolution underlined the right of government employees to work in the language of their choice. The resolution was aimed at implementing the recommendations of the Commission, but also at trying to solve a problem raised in the report. Inequality between French and English workers existed, so by allowing employees to work regardless of their language, it broke down the centuries-old barrier to advancement that French Canadians had to deal with on a daily basis. Language equality was a difficult thing to achieve, and the Official Languages Act was revised to state that both languages should be treated equally in the workplace. The problem experienced in bilingual workplaces was that supervisors were, for the most part, English-speaking, and forms, computer programs and staff communications were usually all in English. So if you were French, you needed to be bilingual, but if you were English, you were not required to learn French.

In Québec, in 1972 and in 1977, French was recognized as the only official language, and the famous *Loi 101* (Bill 101) was enacted. While *Loi 101* was, in essence, a statement that everyone had the right to be served in French, to work in French, and so on, it did spark a debate regarding street signs, which according to the law, had to be in French. Of course, any business that happened to have an English name highlighted the fact that there were problems with this law. After much debate, the law was amended in 1988 to allow for signage in other languages, provided that French was dominant. My husband purchased the rights to a franchise called Play It Again Sports, a brand name. But in order to respect the law, his sign had to be modified to add a French sentence to the logo. For him, just like others who own franchises such as Second Cup or Chapters, or any other name that happens to be in English, the law seems a bit much. Enforcing the law is the responsibility of the Office de la Langue française, created in 1961 with the mission of ensuring the promotion of the French language. Québec is indeed years ahead in terms of the cultural and political protection of French.

Bilingualism is definitely the most significant influence that the French have had on Canada. It is sad that this issue has often been connected with separatism, but it shouldn't be. Having two official languages gives Canada a great advantage and allows Canadians to be fluent in two of the most-spoken languages in the world. It means we can talk about hockey, beer, poutine and politics in two languages— a definite advantage.

CHAPTER EIGHT

THE FRENCH COMMUNITY IN THE MARITIMES

The French community in the Maritimes is mostly of Acadian descent. Acadia was settled in 1604, though this first attempt was disastrous. It was only in the 1630s that colonization of the area took off. In 1713, the territory was ceded to Britain, and this commenced the sad epic of the Acadians. The British required that the Acadians swear allegiance to their government, which is usually what colonies are expected to do. What this allegiance meant, though, was that if the motherland entered into a conflict and needed troops, money or weapons, its colonies were expected to contribute. The Acadians refused to do so because they had no reason to—no relationship with England, no desire to participate in any type of conflict. To avoid any problems, Acadians decided to remain neutral, which meant they wouldn't fight for England, but wouldn't fight against it, either. This seemed like a pretty good place to be in and a pretty good deal for the British.

Acadia's stance was tolerated for a while, but ultimately the British, in the person of Governor Charles Lawrence, decided to end the special status of the Acadians. I guess neutrality was not good enough for the British—making a verbal promise to serve the king was important. This shows how things have changed—a verbal promise for anything today would not stand a chance. Lawrence issued a declaration that was passed in the Council of Nova Scotia in July 1755 stating:

> After mature consideration it was unanimously agreed, that, to prevent as much as possible their attempting to return and molest the settlers that may be set down on their lands, it would be most proper to send them to be distributed amongst the several colonies on the continent, and that a sufficient number of vessels should be hired with all possible expedition for that purpose.

The deportation, or *Grand Dérangement* (Great Upheaval), of 1755 happened rapidly, leaving barely any time for people to escape. Once the Acadians had been herded onto boats, their land and crops were torched, reminiscent of the kind of thing the French did to Native populations. There were rumours that Lawrence actually made money with his "great idea." By sending the Acadians away, he allegedly pocketed money from the sale of their estates and cattle (whatever had not been burned). But an investigation was carried out by one of his colleagues, and his name was (unsurprisingly) cleared of any charges. In 1762, Lawrence's successor, Jonathan Belcher, was still trying to send Acadians away, those who had managed to escape deportation a few years earlier. That's perseverance gone awfully wrong.

The worst part of the deportation story was that the Acadians were not all sent to one place—many were deported to Maine, Virginia and Georgia, some elsewhere in Canada and some even to France, where they felt completely out of place. Of the more than 10,000 Acadians who were deported, divided from their families, and ripped from their homes, close to 10 percent died because their ships sank or because of diseases they caught on the boats.

There was no time to dwell on how tragic the event was because the Seven Years' War began shortly afterwards, ending in the conquest of New France in 1760. The Acadians were gone, and French Canadian territory now belonged to the British. Wherever the Acadians landed in Canada or in the American colonies, the place was inevitably in a state of war, which means that the little help they might have received was even harder to obtain. The Acadians spoke French and were Catholics, and as such, they were easily pinpointed as exiles, making their inclusion in their new society that much more difficult.

Upon their arrival in the United States, the Acadians usually became the responsibility of whatever organization cared for the poor. For people who previously had been relatively well-off landowners, this was a drastic change in their social status. The Acadians must have felt unwanted wherever they went—they could not provide for themselves because they didn't speak the language, their home country was now completely under British control, and the government overseeing their new home tried to get rid of them in anyway it could. For example, in 1764, there was an invitation issued for all Acadians living in New England to pack up their stuff and go to Santo Domingo, where they could get a piece of land. The offer was similar to indenture and represented a way to get rid of the Acadians while at the same time sending them somewhere they could be profitable to the American government. The "deal" required the Acadians to work for a certain amount of time before they could receive the piece of land they had been promised. In any case, Acadians held onto their culture, their religion and their language and tried as best they could to fit in wherever they were. Some were finally allowed to return to Canada, but they established themselves in New Brunswick rather than Nova Scotia. By the 19th century, there were some 10,000 Acadians in the Maritimes; by the time of Confederation, their numbers had grown to 87,000.

After the shock and sadness of deportation, Acadians began coming back many years later, sparking what has been called an "Acadian renaissance" in the second half of the 19th century. Many settled in Clare, Nova Scotia, and this area is still known as *la ville française*, the French town. Anglophones tend to refer to this area as the French coast, which sounds more exotic. Clare is now home to more than 7000 Acadians, while more than 250,000 Acadians are said to live in the rest of Canada. Interestingly, the cradle of French in the Maritimes, Nova Scotia, is not bilingual, and Acadians have had to fight for language rights since their return.

In 1836, an Acadian was elected to the provincial legislative assembly, a first step in getting the Acadians acknowledged as important political players. Simon D'Entremont created an uproar on his first day at work by refusing to take the oath of office. Apparently, the oath had long been abolished, but Catholics still had to take it, perhaps to guarantee that political beliefs would take precedence over any religious issues. In any case, the first Acadian elected to office really took his role seriously… and demonstrated how much Acadians don't like taking oaths.

In 1864, a priest named Camille Lefebvre founded St. Joseph's College in Memramcook, New Brunswick—the first college to open after the Acadian renaissance. It gained prestige fairly quickly, as the Acadian elite elected it as their place of education. The predecessor of the Université de Moncton, it hosted the first Acadian convention in 1881. Education in French was at the forefront of the Acadians' demands and caused tension between them and their English counterparts. In the 1860s, the Commons Schools Act had slowly eroded the French Catholic school system. It was forbidden to teach in French or to teach about the Catholic religion. In 1875, in Caraquet, this led indirectly to a series of skirmishes now known as the Caraquet riots. One probable cause was the election to the school board of Théotime Blanchard. As a protest against the School Act, he decided not to pay his dues to the board, but because he was an elected official, this was awkward for some English-speaking members, too. Things escalated to the point where a small group of Francophones barged into the office of one of the men who had complained about the situation and began to yell and throw papers at him. The relatively minor skirmish rapidly degenerated into street rioting and unfortunately resulted in the shooting of two of the rioters. Education, as we will see in Chapter 10, is one of the basic rights that French Canadians have fought for and secured for themselves, or are still trying to secure. Today, Université Ste-Anne offers education in French, and there is a French school board bearing the name Conseil scolaire Acadien.

As was mentioned earlier, the first Acadian convention was organized in 1881 and was held at St. Joseph's College. The event attracted some 5000 Acadians from across the continent, and the conference inaugurated an official Acadian "birthday," to be celebrated annually on August 15. Even though St. Jean Baptiste was supposed to be the unifying day for all Francophones in Canada, it was decided at the convention that the story of the Acadians was too different to be celebrated on the same day.

A subsequent convention in 1884 adopted an official flag for the Acadian nation (similar to the French flag but sporting a gold star), and attendees decided on an official motto, which was *L'union fait la force* (Strength through unity).

During this second convention, which was held in PEI, an Acadian hymn became the rallying cry for the dispersed Acadians. Here are some of the lyrics:

Acadie, ma patrie
À ton nom, je me lie
Ma vie, ma foi sont à toi
Tu me protégeras.

Acadie, ma patrie
Ma terre et mon défi
De près, de loin tu me tiens
Mon coeur est acadien.

Acadie, ma patrie
Ton histoire, je la vis
La fierté, je te la dois
En l'avenir, je crois.

English translation:

Acadia, my homeland
To your name I draw myself
My life, my faith belong to you
You will protect me.

Acadia, my homeland
My land and my challenge
From near, from far you hold onto me
My heart is Acadian.

Acadia, my homeland
I live your history
I owe you my pride
I believe in your future.

Since 1994, a World Acadian Congress has been held every five years, an idea of André Boudreau, an Acadian from Alberta. The Congress tries to reach out to Acadian communities far away, such as that in Louisiana. When talking about the French influence in Canada, it seems unfair to leave out Louisiana because of a border. At one time part of the territory of New France, Louisiana is a true testament to the French influence on the continent, the one and only French bastion in the sea of English-speaking Americans. Just like Québec, this state held onto its particular language and culture, though the language is, of course, much less protected in the U.S.

The Cajuns are an important part of Louisiana culture, and the word Cajun is derived from the French word *Acadien*, or its short version, *'Cadien*. Two theories have been proposed for the origin of the word Cajun. The name was possibly an insult, a way to underline that the *'Cadiens* belonged to a lower social stratum. The other, less pessimistic theory is that English-speaking people could not pronounce *Acadiens*, and the word simply changed over the years. Either way, the French influence is felt across the United States, in a country that has only one official language and does not guarantee language rights to anyone else.

About 100 years after the Acadian expulsion, 1847 to be exact, a poem called "Evangeline," written by American poet Henry Wadsworth Longfellow, was published. The poem voices the plight of two lovers caught in the whirlwind of deportation who lose each other on the eve of their wedding:

> Many a year had passed since the
>   burning of Grand Pré
> When on the falling tide the freighted
>   vessels departed
> Bearing a nation, with all its household
>   gods, into exile,
> Exile without an end, and without
>   an example in story.
> Far asunder, on separate coasts,
>   the Acadians landed;
> Scattered were they, like flakes of snow,
>   when the wind from the north-east
> Strikes aslant through the fogs that
>   darken the banks of Newfoundland.

The fictional story was a tremendous success, and it created awareness of the Acadians' history. Evangeline soon became a somewhat mythical figure—readers everywhere were enthralled by the story and wanted to visit its enchanting setting. The fact that Evangeline never existed didn't matter. The tourism industry of Nova Scotia began using Evangeline as a selling point, although the idealized country life that people came to experience did not really exist. For example, farmers tilling the land felt awkward having groups of people staring at them because of a poem. Tourists would come to look for Evangeline's grave or the house she grew up in, and it became difficult to get people to understand that she was really just an invention. The character of Evangeline came to represent Acadia after the poem was published in the mid-19th century, even though she had been created by an American and thus might not have been representative of Nova Scotia's Acadians.

In 1971, another fictional character became the new flagbearer of the Acadian nation—La Sagouine, a character created by Acadian author Antonine Maillet. The novel *La Sagouine* is the story of a washerwoman in rural PEI in the early 20th century. This book stands out because it was written in Chiac, the Acadian dialect that is a combination of English and French. The novel presented the language to the Canadian public and has inspired tourist sightseeing expeditions just like the poem "Evangeline" did. Indeed, you can see Le Pays de la Sagouine, a theme park based on the book and showcasing Acadian culture, if you visit Bouctouche, New Brunswick. The novel was transformed into a play shortly after its publication and became a TV series in 1977. The series was relaunched two years ago as a DVD set, proof that the character has stood the test of time.

CHAPTER NINE

THE FRENCH
COMMUNITY IN QUÉBEC

Québec is perhaps the most obvious legacy of the French. Québeckers proudly compare themselves to the Gaulois in the French *Astérix* comics. The comics portray a small community fighting against the mighty Romans in the pre-Christian era, so the comparison is in the sense of David versus Goliath, or in this case, the French versus the English. *La belle province* has managed to keep its language and culture alive despite being surrounded by Anglophone provinces and infiltrated by English-speaking Québeckers. Following a conquest that should have ended the French way of life, Québec residents have held onto their right to practice their religion and speak their language. After the Conquest of 1760 and much fighting (in the streets and in Parliament), French Canadians were able to abolish the seigneurial system, at least on paper. This system had grown disadvantageous for French Canadians, who were forced to work for *seigneurs* who were now British. And by 1860, the whole idea of working for someone just to be able to have a home was becoming a bit outdated. Another fight that French Canadians took on, and won, was the right to be educated in French. The most educated French Canadians, who happened to be Catholic priests and nuns, were the teachers. Because the Church had become more and more powerful since the days of Maisonneuve and his Ville-Marie, education was provided by the different religious orders and was obligatory.

These small victories did not come easy, as the rebellions of 1837–38 can testify. After experiencing a cholera epidemic and severe agricultural difficulties, discontent grew among French Canadians, who blamed the English government for their situation. Blaming the English was certainly the first reflex and, at that time, perhaps they were indeed the ones mostly responsible for the French Canadians' problems. A decade after the rebellions in Québec, the English were blamed for the miseries of yet another people, the Irish. The Potato Famine of the 1840s in Ireland was blamed on the English, who didn't help enough when they could have. It seems the problem in Québec was similar, though not as dramatic. Cholera and the bad weather were natural problems, but people who were in the middle of it had the feeling that nothing was being done to help. Adding to the problem was that the French Canadians had been conquered by a people they had learned to despise. Louis-Joseph Papineau decided to voice these feelings of resentment, and he took part in the formation of a group called *les Patriotes*. They had several demands for the British government, which they summarized into a document called the 92 Resolutions. If the 92 resolutions were a just a summary of their demands, the original document must have been massive.

Among other requests, the men asked that a) the seignieurial system finally be abolished, b) their rights and language be respected, c) more political power be given to the Québec Assembly and d) more representation be given to French Canadians in governmental staffing. These demands were all refused, which caused a public uproar. A disorganized rebellion followed, some of it taking place in Québec, but there was also rioting in Upper Canada. What happened in Québec resulted in the hanging of 12 of the participants and the deportation to Australia of several others. The event, in the end, actually went against Papineau's beliefs.

Indeed, he believed in non-violent action and escaped to the United States when the movement he initiated became an outright rebellion. Narratives of this event made Papineau into a martyr, exiled to the States because he fought for the rights of French Canadians, when, in fact, he simply wanted to protest by legal means and left when he saw how radical the situation had become. Rebellion means rejecting the existing order, while Papineau's wish was to use the existing system in order to obtain certain rights by legal and political means. In fact, what Papineau requested most in his 92 resolutions was to have more political power, not to question authority.

Papineau did not approve of violence at all, let alone outright rebellion. He was actually challenged several times to duels by men he had offended, but he refused every time. These invitations usually came after public declarations were published in *La Minerve*, a newspaper created primarily to disseminate Papineau's ideas and discontent. According to some, Papineau might have been a bit of a crook. He apparently told many people that he had never participated in the rebellion although it was easy to prove that he did. In fact, he had been supreme commander of a unit right before he escaped. Then again, the rebellion was seen differently at different points in time, which meant that it was sometimes a good thing to hide one's participation, and other times it was cool to mention it.

The *Patriotes* of 1837 are mythical figures in Québec, symbols of the constant fight of the French against the English hegemony in the province. In 2002, then-leader of the Parti Québécois, Bernard Landry, announced that a day in May, previously named Dollard Day, would commemorate the rebellion and the fight of the *Patriotes*. This day in May is what other Canadians call Victoria Day.

Dollard des Ormeaux, in whose honour the holiday was previously celebrated, is a Québec hero who has been both celebrated and vilified, depending on the political climate and the historical findings at any given time. The narrative of a skirmish in Long Sault, Ontario, was rediscovered in old documents and mentioned in a book as part of the history of Canada. This was in the 19th century, when history books were written in ornate language and narratives were exaggerated into fantastic stories. The narrative told the magnificent story of a group of men, with Dollard as their leader, who were able, despite their very small number, to fend off a vicious Iroquois attack, though they ended up dying for their cause.

The early (and embellished) account reported that Dollard and his men embarked on an expedition to face the Iroquois, who they knew were coming, in order to save the colony. The story illustrated in detail how brave a man had to be to voluntarily meet the Iroquois, who at this point in history were considered the scariest Natives ever. Other documents were found and further analysis seemed to demonstrate to some extent that the expedition's purpose was, in fact, to obtain furs from the Iroquois in an illegal manner, not to actually fight them. The group might have known the Natives were coming, but considering the former facts, this newer version made Dollard seem much less heroic. Another historian then argued that Dollard had prepared his expedition poorly, which did more harm than good to the colony. In that version, regardless of the reason for the expedition itself, it seems that it was prepared hastily, without a) including enough men to be able to fight off any Natives they might encounter, b) bringing enough weapons to fight off said Natives and c) getting as much information as possible before leaving. Because of the change in the story, Dollard Day had no weight in comparison to the story of the *Patriotes* and lost its annual recognition. The *Patriotes* narrative only got better with time, and even if we know that Papineau did not want to take part in the rebellion, the rest of the participants make the event a cornerstone of Québec history.

The post-Conquest development of Québec was tremendously uneven, as Anglophones grew wealthier and French Canadians struggled to make ends meet. The language difference was a real barrier to advancement for the *habitants*. The business world was developing, immigration numbers were growing, and all this meant that English was becoming the primary language in Québec, whether for doing business or simply for speaking with neighbours. A clear separation formed within the city of Montréal, as the western part of city, the wealthiest, was occupied by the English, and the eastern part by the French, with St. Laurent Street to delineate the "territories." The separation still exists, and people have since developed a sense of belonging according to where they live. For example, the West Island of Montréal, where I live, is primarily Anglophone, and people feel attached to their municipality and what it represents. Beaconsfield is known as a community occupied by the wealthy, so people living there are proud. This also goes for Montréalers living in the East End, like most of my family, who have grown up there and feel that they know the area inside out.

A similar structure existed in the rest of the province because French Canadians lived, for the most part, in rural areas, while the English population chose to live mostly in the cities.

French communities were generally relatively isolated, and there was no incentive to go work in the city because without being able to speak English, there was no hope of finding a job. The English-speaking population seemed to fare better in terms of their income, and related to that, their education, their employment and their industry. The French language, although it was something of a rallying cry among Francophones, was also a way to filter out the French from potential employment. As for religion, it was not so much Roman Catholicism that slowed down French Canadians, but rather it was the hold of the Catholic Church on the educational system. Indeed, the French-language programs were far from state-of-the-art business theories and other subjects that might have been worth learning. My father remembers having to learn Latin when he was young (and he's only 58 years old). Although I can see why someone wanting to study history (like me) could benefit from learning Latin, it seemed absolutely irrelevant for a majority of Québec school children during the 1950s. In the Church's opinion, changes in society were not good because they challenged the Church, and education evolved in the same frame of mind. Both language and religion, the two things the French held onto after the Conquest, were actually slowing them down. I'll bet they didn't see that one coming.

The stranglehold of the Catholic Church was a bit of a problem for the community's development, since the Church had firm control over all aspects of life. The Church feared change because it meant potential loss of power. It was only in the '60s, during what we now call the Quiet Revolution, that the French population of Québec really started to speak up. By Quiet Revolution, we mean the slow and peaceful process by which Québec secularized itself, increased awareness of the inequalities not only between the French and the English, but also between men and women. Québec is the only province in which women are not allowed to take their husband's name after marriage. In fact, since I was born in Québec, and even if I lived all my life in Ontario using my husband's name, the day I stepped back into Québec, I would be required to use my maiden name. The Quiet Revolution encouraged French Canadians to detach themselves from the Church, which meant that only language would hold them together.

Québec was, at the time, trying to get out of what we now call the *Grande Noirceur*, or Great Darkness, which corresponds to the period when Maurice Duplessis was in power. A conservative politician, Duplessis was as retroactive as the Church. He believed in a concept called *la survivance*, which asked French people to gather together and centre their lives around family and land, that is, to try to live like their ancestors. While the idea of staying together to survive seemed logical, it also closed the French community to outside influence and, by extension, progress.

Duplessis left two legacies that Québeckers remember well, one positive and the other negative. He was responsible for the adoption of the Québec flag, the *fleur-de-lysée*. On the other hand, his name is associated with a historical scandal—the Duplessis orphans. With approval from Duplessis, orphans were falsely declared mentally ill so that the government could place them in institutions rather than keeping them in orphanages. Why? Because mental institutions were funded by the government of Canada, while orphanages were paid for by the government of Québec. By declaring the children mentally ill, the Québec government did not have to pay for their subsistence. A fairly large-scale scandal ensued, but it was not the last time that federal money would be used for something other than what was declared. From what I can recall, a certain case of sponsorship made the news fairly recently, and our former Governor General has had to justify some $400,000 spent on who knows what. Maybe the scandal was worse because it was the first to come to light, or perhaps because Duplessis already had a bad reputation. If his régime was called the

Great Darkness, he surely wasn't liked that much.

With the election of Jean Lesage in 1960, the revolution began, through the enactment of various laws and regulations that helped the development of French Canadian society and culture. One of the most effective changes was to take health care and education away from the Church and put it under government control instead. Since the Church had slowed down French Canadians, it needed to be cast aside. It is also because of Lesage that Québec has become the most taxed province in Canada—an accomplishment that I am sure Québeckers are thankful for. Who doesn't like to pay more taxes?

The Quiet Revolution ended with a bang (no pun intended) with the October Crisis of 1970. The crisis was caused by a group called the FLQ, the Front de Libération du Québec (Québec Liberation Front). The FLQ had a knack for making bombs and decided to put this talent to use, exploding close to 100 bombs, most of them in mailboxes in wealthy Anglophone areas of Montréal, Westmount in particular. This in itself would have been an entertaining episode in French Canadian history (and postal history), but things turned ugly quickly. FLQ members exploded a bomb in the Stock Exchange, injuring 27 people, and they kidnapped two politicians, James Cross, a British diplomat, and Pierre Laporte, the Québec Minister of Labour, eventually murdering Laporte. Their terrorist actions frightened people, and Prime Minister Pierre Elliott Trudeau decided invoke the War Measures Act to stop the madness. This Act revoked, temporarily, the civil rights of Québeckers, and the government was allowed to arrest anyone they suspected to be part of the FLQ. In the end, the FLQ was stopped, and things eventually went back to normal. Even mailboxes were left alone. The October Crisis marked the end of the Quiet Revolution simply because, well, that crisis was not very quiet.

Although the Quiet Revolution ended with exploding mailboxes, it supposedly started with a riot caused by a hockey player. This in itself is so Canadian, it almost seems invented. In my master's thesis, I studied Maurice Richard, a hockey player nicknamed "The Rocket," who has since been mythicized to the point that he was, and still is, sometimes credited for starting the Quiet Revolution. How does a hockey player start a social revolution, you might ask? Well, in 1955, it was announced that the Rocket was suspended for the season for breaking a hockey stick over a referee's back. Because Richard was the star player for the Montréal Canadiens, also called the Habs (for *habitants*), it was unlikely that the team would be able to win the Stanley Cup. Richard sometimes scored up to five goals in a single game, which helped the team achieve its impressive ranking.

The evening following this dreadful announcement, people gathered at the Montréal Forum to protest the suspension. These people were angry, but not as angry as the those who actually attended the game that night and ended up being evacuated from the building. The fans inside had been busy throwing food at Clarence Campbell, the man responsible for the suspension. During the shortened game, he was pelted with eggs, lettuce, tomatoes and enough other ingredients to make himself a good sandwich. Someone also threw a non-edible thing at Campbell, tear gas, forcing the Montréal Police to evacuate the building and cancel the game. The situation snowballed into a full-blown riot, costing more than $100,000 in damages and continuing well into the early hours of the morning.

While the riot was said to have been caused by irate fans of the team, it was soon interpreted as a revolt of the French (with Richard as the flagbearer) against the hold of the Anglophones on society (represented by the mostly English management of the National Hockey League). The fact that Clarence Campbell was the one who had made the decision to suspend the Rocket made everything worse.

Campbell represented the way the French saw the English—raised in a wealthy family, he was well educated, while Richard had no education and struggled to make ends meet. The conflict between the two seemed to resemble the battle between the French and the English, which is why the riot became such a hyped event. This riot is now said to be one of the first stands taken by the French community to voice its discontent with the society of the time.

So, following a mailbox bomb crisis and a hockey riot, things were bound to change. In 1976, the election of the Parti Québécois with René Lévesque as premier of Québec marked the beginning of the movement for separation. Separatism means that some French Québeckers wish to be separated from the rest of Canada as a means of protecting the French culture and language. Of course, given the geographical position of the province, separatism also means cutting up the country, which most Canadians are against. It also means that the English-speaking minority living in Québec would end up in a French-speaking country. Actually, when the Parti Québécois became the province's leading party, a great number of Anglophones moved to Ontario, mostly to Toronto. Two referendums were passed asking if Québec's population was willing to separate, and both times, the No side won. Actually, the first time, Yes meant that you were for separation, and for the same thing, you had to answer No to the second referendum question. So, Yes won, but it really meant No. Confusing? In fact, many people complained that the question was so complicated that they were not sure what they were really answering.

In 1980, the difference between the two sides was marked (60 percent against separation and 40 percent for), and its instigator, René Lévesque, responded to the defeat by telling everyone that they would succeed the next time. As promised, 15 years later there was another referendum, and the margin was paper-thin: 50.58 percent against separation and 49.42 percent for. Jacques Parizeau, head of the Parti Québécois at the time, was not as graceful about the defeat and blamed immigrants for the loss, a statement that killed his political career. Even today, the wish for sovereignty is vibrant, and the subject is always on the table in Québec. But the Parti Québécois, now called the Bloc Québécois, can be remembered for some positive actions, for example, the Charter of the French Language, which made French the official language of the province. It also changed the licence plate motto.

It is widely believed that the licence plate slogan *Je me souviens* (I remember), the Québec motto, fell a tad on the revenge side of things, maybe because of two failed referendums. The phrase can almost be seen as threatening the English conquerors, something along the line of "I remember what you have done"—kind of like the scary movie *I Know What You Did Last Summer*. The slogan was adopted in 1978 and replaced the previous one of *La belle province*, which is now a very successful chain of fast-food restaurants. Eugène-Étienne Taché, a French Canadian who had worked on plans for the façade of a legislative building, has been credited for our current licence plate inscription because he set up these words in a coat of arms for a building he was working on.

It was "discovered" in 1991 that the motto was actually part of a poem by Taché, which goes as follows: *Je me souviens d'être né sous le lys et d'avoir grandit sous la rose* (I remember being born under the lily and growing up under the rose). This, of course, was huge— the motto Québeckers had been flaunting as an angry guilt trip was actually saying that, while we remembered our French roots, we were able to grow as a nation because of the British, as the flowers respectively correspond to the two countries' symbols. This was questioned as well, as some did not believe that the first line of *Je me souviens* actually belonged with the rest of the poem. All in all, it seems that some agree that the Québec motto does not have any deeper meaning than to say that we remember our history, rather than an angry message or a secret meaning *à la Da Vinci Code*. Nevertheless, the licence plate has been the subject of many debates, just like anything of symbolic value.

CHAPTER TEN

THE FRENCH COMMUNITY IN ONTARIO

Ontario was first colonized by the French as part of the expansion movement towards the end of the 17th century, was most of the territory to the west of Québec. By 1701, the first agricultural colony in southern Ontario was being established at Fort Pontchartrain (Detroit). In Eastern Ontario, the real boost to the development of the region's French community stemmed from the founding of the Ottawa diocese in 1847. The overpopulation of Québec's parishes encouraged people to seek new homes in this area. The French Canadians soon formed the largest minority group. Today, Ottawa is still the most important French community in Ontario.

The first immigration movements were motivated by employment in the timber industry. In the 19th century, wood was a staple trade product for Canada. Large pieces of lumber were sent to Britain, where they were cut up into smaller pieces and sold. One of the most important markets for Canadian wood was the Royal Navy, which ordered its huge masts from Canada. The U.S. and the West Indies eventually became customers as well. Lumber was one of the first important Canadian industries, and thus one that employed a lot of people right away. French Canadians had been living in the woods for centuries, so it seemed only natural that they had become experts at cutting it, too. But forests were becoming scarce in Québec, at least in terms of massive timber to cut, and the search for new forests (and work) pushed the limits of the territory to Ontario and beyond. French Canadians moved to these new places looking for work, along with many other immigrant groups. Little villages were established by and for lumberjacks, and all was well until fights erupted between the different groups of immigrants, all there for the same reason—to work. Fights occurred, of course, between the different nationalities but also between French-speaking and English-speaking workers.

Jos (Joseph) Montferrand remains a somewhat mythical figure in the area because he defend the cause of the French Canadians and fought with them against the English-speaking bullies. Montferrand was a strong man who had already made the news by the time he was 16 years old. He attended a boxing match in Montréal, and when the commentator invited people to challenge one of the boxers who had just fought, Montferrand volunteered and apparently knocked the boxer right out. A giant for the time at 6'4", Jos was born in Montréal and did what many of his neighbours did—he left town and went to work in the Ottawa region first as a *voyageur* for the Hudson's Bay Company and then as a logger. Animosity came to a boil between Irish immigrants and the Francophone population in 1829. In an area called Shiners, where Irish bullies gave the French Canadians a hard time, Montferrand supposedly fought off a gang of 150 Irish loggers. While the story is undoubtedly exaggerated (I mean, who can really fight 150 people?), but what it tells us is that a) the man was strong as a horse, and b) he fought like a madman. The moral of the story was perhaps that French Canadians were outsiders as much as the newly arrived Irish or Scottish workers. They had to fight as often as other immigrants did and had no advantage because they came from the neighbouring province.

In Northern Ontario, French immigration started around the mid-19th century with the construction of railways, not only the Canadian Pacific Railway (CPR), but also a line linking Northern and Southern Ontario. While immigrants seemed to have built the railways of Canada, the French quickly learned how to use the new mode of transportation. The Canadian mining and lumber industries were what enticed French immigrants to move so far away from their roots. Most of the French immigrants came from Québec and were searching for better employment opportunities. With the growing population of Québec, the job market was saturated and the prospect of secure employment and better pay in Ontario mines, forest and industrial areas was quite a draw. The great number of Frenchmen coming to newly opened territories meant that they sometimes became the main population in newly established mining or lumbering villages. This explains why cities such as Sudbury had a predominantly Francophone population even though they were surrounded by English-speaking towns.

The case of Toronto in Southern Ontario is a particular story. Back in the early 16th century, Toronto was on the route between Lake Ontario and Lake Huron. In 1615, Frenchman Étienne Brûlé arrived in the area. He was the first European in Ontario and also the first *coureur des bois*. Several schools in Toronto bear his name because his visit to Ontario apparently ended right on the site of the future economic capital. What a lucky stop that was. Born in Paris, Brûlé is believed to have been part of Champlain's expedition. Well versed in the Huron language, he became Champlain's interpreter. After he was blamed for the conquest of the territory by the Kirke brothers, Brûlé decided to leave white society and go live with the Hurons. For reasons that are not known today, Brûlé was killed by members of his new community in the 1630s. His tragic end has, of course, added to his peculiar story as the first white man to see Ontario. There were speculations that perhaps Brûlé was eaten by his adopted tribe, but no proof has ever been found. Given that his name means "burnt" in French, if he was indeed eaten, he was definitely not a happy meal.

Toronto is an Anglophone city, no doubt about it. A book on the Francophone population in the Greater Toronto Area titled *The Invisible French* illustrates very effectively that French Canadians are a rare sight around the CN Tower. Nevertheless, there are French-speaking communities, and they've been organized for a long time—the first Catholic Church service in the city was recorded in 1797–98. A French parish, Sacré-Coeur, was established in 1887, and its church still offers services in French. In Toronto, just like almost everywhere else in Ontario, the French are not concentrated in a specific area but can be found throughout the city. Because of the proximity of Ontario to Québec, the French did not feel like immigrants and did not feel the need to congregate in small societies to form sort of a village within a village. Instead, they adapted to their new environment, which explains why the proportion of French Canadians who actually speak French is decreasing every year. The French culture is still in evidence, and the 70-something French restaurants in downtown Toronto testify to its importance, even in Canada's economic capital. Another remnant is the French theatre in the city, which opened in 1967 under the name Théâtre du Petit Bonheur and is now called the Théâtre Français. The long life of this cultural establishment demonstrates that there is indeed a French population that wishes to attend venues in French. In fact, this theatre is the longest running one in Canada outside the province of Québec.

At the start, three languages were allowed as educational languages in Ontario: French, English and German. However, by 1912, through Regulation 17, the use of French was forbidden in schools, and I assume that German did not last too long, either, certainly not past World War II. The creation of Francophone education associations (for example, the Association canadienne-française d'éducation d'Ontario, guided by the Catholic Church of

Ontario) followed shortly and started lobbying in favour of a bilingual educational system. Fifteen years later, the regulation was amended thanks to their good work—bills 140 and 141 called for complete programs in either bilingual or French-only secondary schools. The 1969 law proclaiming the equality of both languages brought about the financing of French education in Ontario and thus allowed more programs to be developed. Today, many Ontario schools offer education in both languages. For example, the University of Ottawa and Laurentian University offer complete programs of study in French. The University of Ottawa was originally a Catholic university, founded in 1848 by the Oblates of Marie-Immaculée, but it became secular in 1965. Until the 1960s, it was the only university outside Québec that granted diplomas for French programs. Among the many Canadian personalities who were able to show off their Ottawa diplomas were Louis-Adolphe Olivier, the first Franco-Ontarian judge, and Bernadette Tarte, one of the first non-Catholic women to get a university diploma. The university has awarded honorary degrees to Margaret Trudeau, wife of former Prime Minister Pierre Trudeau, as well as King Hussein of Jordan. This demonstrates how the university has grown from a small college to an internationally recognized university. The University of Ottawa is part of an association of

Canadian Francophone universities, along with College Universitaire de St. Boniface, Campus St. Jean of the University of Alberta, the University of Moncton and Laurentian University, among others.

Laurentian University is situated in Sudbury and was founded in 1957, originally as a Jesuit college. In 1975, the flag of the Franco-Ontarian community, created by one of the university's history teachers, was first raised on its campus. Laurentian University, just like its host city of Sudbury, was important to the development of French culture in Ontario. Sudbury is a great example of how the French influence is still alive throughout Canada. My husband is originally from Sudbury and spoke French as a child, only learning English when he moved to Montréal. His family, the Lalonde clan of Sudbury, Coniston and environs, seems to me to be representative of the Francophones in Ontario—though they speak English most of the time, they are extremely proud of their French origins. When they found out that I was French Canadian, and when I finally visited Sudbury to attend a wedding, I was in for a surprise. Although I spoke to the Lalondes and Dubies in English, they made a point of responding in French and pronouncing my name in French.

Boasting a population that is 28 percent French-speaking and 40 percent bilingual today, Sudbury began as a nickel and copper mining town in the 1880s, when the CPR line reached the area. Even today, it advertises itself as the Mining Capital of Canada and organizes celebrations with mining at their core.

The first area to be developed outside the original settlement was called Moulin à fleur, a name taken from an old flour mill, which is still standing. Beginning as a slum for poor miners in the late 19th century, its status and look changed as the pay and status of the miners increased. Sudbury was initially called the Ste-Anne des Pins parish. Way before the CPR arrived on the scene, the parish priest had the material for building the church placed on a raft to take it to its uncharted destination.

Sudbury has produced many influential Canadians: Paul Desmarais, a Canadian financier and the fifth richest man in Canada; Robert Campeau, a real estate developer; Conrad Lavigne, a television broadcaster who started the first French-language radio station outside Québec; and André Paiement, a successful musician and playwright.

Paiement had a great influence on the cultural development of the Franco-Ontarian community. He contributed to the creation of CANO, the Coopérative des artistes du Nouvel Ontario, which itself inspired other cultural enterprises. For example, Paiement and CANO helped create the Théâtre du Nouvel Ontario, the publishing company Prise de parole, the Franco-Ontarian institute, and another CANO, that one a band. CANO truly changed the culture of Nouvel Ontario (a name used originally by both the French and the English to describe the more developed area of Northern Ontario), and made Sudbury its regional capital. The energy that helped achieve all of these cultural projects in the 1970s can be explained very simply—the largest wave of Québec-Ontario immigration took place during that time. Paiement had a hand in pretty much all of these things, devoting his life to this cultural development. He committed suicide in 1978, but before he died, he was able to show how difficult life was for Franco-Ontarians. In a ballet adaptation of a play by Molière, work that he titled *Schizophrénie*, Paiement at one point says:

> Schizophrénie! Schizophrénie!
> You will bien vouloir excuser
> Our manière de parler
> Mais nous comprenons what we say
>   Schizophrénie!
> Schizophrénie is what we be.

English translation:

Schizophrenia! Schizophrenia!
You will excuse
Our way of speaking
But we understand what we say
    Schizophrenia!
Schizophrenia is what we be.

This particular quotation uses the language we call Frenglish, a widely used combination of both French and English. My humble translation sounds awful, I know, but it is literally what is being said here. Frenglish is really an interesting way to speak. It basically shows that our lives are divided between the two languages, and we use whatever words come to our head first, whether they are English or French. This particular quotation talks about the schizophrenia of being both English and French in a very imaginative way. Although Paiment died prematurely, he accomplished a great deal for the Franco-Ontarian community.

Since 1973, Sudbury has organized an annual music festival called *La Nuit sur l'étang* (literally, "A Night on the Pond"), another project to which Paiement contributed that promotes the cultural vitality of the Francophone community in Northern Ontario. This was all part of a Quiet Revolution in Ontario, which focused on promoting culture and language rather than voicing political demands. Mostly, it was an artistic revolution, as we see in the creation of all these cultural institutions.

Today, Ontario remains an important example of the French influence in Canada. Many of its cities are as proudly bilingual as those in Québec. I went to Ottawa for a television show and, as a first-timer in the capital, was amazed that throughout my stay, I was first addressed in French. It is the same for many other Ontario cities, such as Hawkesbury and Sudbury, and this is really an illustration of how important the French were in Ontario's history and how important they are now. As I mentioned before, the Lalonde family in Sudbury, Coniston and the like have made me realize how proud one should be of one's French roots.

Chapter Eleven

The French Community on the Prairies

The largest French community on the Prairies is found in Alberta, while Saskatchewan hosts the smallest. French immigration dates back to the 1730s and continued during the post-Conquest rush to find a sea passage to the east and new fur territories. The first recorded presence was Pierre Gauthier de la Vérendrye, who established trading posts on the Red River, Assiniboine River and Saskatoon River. La Vérendrye is an important part of the history of the Prairies as he was the first European to see the territory. There is a monument in St. Boniface, Manitoba, dedicated to him. He was really the one who pushed for exploration under the mandate of expanding the fur market, and he encouraged competition against the Hudson's Bay Company's monopoly on the fur trade. His expeditions to western Canada were truly what opened up the territory, and the explorers and settlers that followed did the rest. His accomplishments were not appreciated back in Montréal, and it took some time before he was recognized as one of the great Frenchmen in Canadian history. The reason was pretty simple—La Vérendrye was exploring Canada through funding from French companies. These companies were expecting La Vérendrye to return with tons of furs as payback, but their expectations never materialized. I guess if you pay someone to go get you something, you expect the person to come back with the goods. People did not really care how far he went inland if there were no concrete financial advantages. In a way, he contributed to the founding of Manitoba, developing strong and positive relations with the Natives, which enabled the founding of settlements and the further development of the colony. But getting along with the Natives was not a primary goal for the new Canadians—they wanted furs, not friends.

The French Canadians who immigrated to the Prairies worked mostly in the fur industry, manning the trading posts and transporting furs to eastern posts. Because of the distance between Québec and the new trading posts, many fur traders took Native wives, giving birth to a nation called the Métis, who spoke French, but also Métis. The *coureurs des bois* took wives from several tribes including the Ojibway, Algonquin and Cree, which meant that all these Native cultures were incorporated with the white European culture. The creation of the Métis people was truly a confirmation of the intertwined destinies of the Natives and the Europeans because the Métis were the direct result of European exploration.

The French Canadians took on one Native clothing habit—that of wearing a sash, called a *ceinture fléchée* in French, which has since been transplanted to Québec. Indeed, the "traditional" Québec *habitant* uniform includes a sash worn around the waist, although it was the Métis of western Canada who really started the custom. The French population throughout the Prairies can be traced to the spread of the Métis people. The clergy was there right at the beginning and was instrumental in the founding of the western colonies and in their development and survival. Father Albert Lacombe learned the Cree language before going deep inland to what would become Alberta. The St. Albert mission is the oldest church in Alberta and represents the passion and devotion of the Oblates in doing missionary work. Lacombe not only learned the Cree language from the Natives, but he also learned their agricultural methods.

He started clearing land as soon as he got there, helping the community to develop rapidly. Father Lacombe also lived in a Blackfoot community for a while. When they were attacked, he almost died; when there was an epidemic, he got just as sick as they did. He seemed to prefer the Native people to his fellow Canadians, who he thought swore too much and got drunk far too often. Canadians still drink and swear, so Father Lacombe would probably not enjoy us today, either.

The clergy is really what united the Francophones from the West, as communities were brought together and organized thanks to Catholic priests. One of the most vivid examples of the Catholic religion helping to build a community is Lac Ste-Anne, where Lacombe learned his Cree before establishing St. Albert. Lac Ste-Anne was, and still is, a place of pilgrimage for both Natives and Catholics, though the Natives call it Spirit Lake (*Manito Sakahigan*). Miracles have been recorded there since the 1880s, and the annual pilgrimage has become one of the largest gatherings of Catholics in western Canada. Victoria Belcourt Calihoo, a Métis woman born in the area in 1861, had 12 children and lived to be 104 years old. She was a descendent of a *coureur des bois* and born from a Native-European union. She married a Métis man, continuing the lineage. In the following quotation from the book

Walking in the Woods: A Métis Journey by Herb Belcourt, she recalls how central the fur trade was to the lives of her people:

> We bartered our furs at the H.B. Co. Usually the Company advanced a settler with credit after haying, and on through the year until the trapper brought in his catch. So much fur for this, so much fur for the other article. Later on, when the Indian Commissioners came to pay treaty money [in the late 1870s and 1880s], money began to circulate. It seemed more confusing to deal in money when one was accustomed to barter. I have heard of some Indians trading a used five-dollar bill for a brand new dollar bill.

The late 19th century was a turning point in Prairie history as the influx of Oblates and their influence on the Métis communities changed the landscape from vast empty territories to populated areas slowly forming into provinces. The French oblates left their names on a number of missions, communities and regions, and helped Canada to become the country it is today.

As seen in Victoria's recollection, the Hudson's Bay Company was very important as well, as it owned the stores where the Métis purchased all their goods using furs as payment.

The HBC also contributed a great deal to the development of the Prairies. The company actually owned the territory that would eventually become western Canada, which the Canadian government eventually purchased from them. At one point, the company was the single largest landowner of the country. Although it was an obvious source of employment, the HBC did not allow Métis employees to advance, and they usually remained in the lower levels of the company. Of course, this situation created discontent among the Métis, seeing as they remained impoverished even though they were employed, while their white counterparts, who spoke English, got wealthy. Another option for a young Métis was to become a independent fur trader, thus bypassing the HBC and annoying the heck out of the big boss, Sir George Simpson.

This went on for a while until Pierre-Guillaume Sayer became an example for all the illegal Métis traders when he was put on trial for his actions. His fellow men all came armed to the opening of the session but only fired the guns for joy when Sayer came out of court a free man. Although he was found guilty of trading illegally, he was neither fined nor charged because the court believed that he genuinely thought his activities were legal. His discharge meant one thing for the Métis—that the fur trade was now deregulated—and this indirectly brought the HBC and its relatively negative hold on the Métis population to a halt. The French Métis had dealt a blow to the almighty HBC, and an era of independent economic development began.

The most notorious Métis was undoubtedly Louis Riel, who formed a provisional provincial government in Manitoba, thus actually creating the province in 1870. The territory had been sold to the Canadian government a year earlier by the Hudson's Bay Company for the sum of $300,000. This enabled the province to begin its life as a bilingual territory, with as many English as French-speaking settlers. Bilingualism in Manitoba did not last long, and in 1890, French was removed as an official language. However, in 1976, it was declared through a ruling of the Supreme Court that the actions of 1890 were, in fact, illegal. This came about because of Georges Forest, a Franco-Manitoban who complained about a parking ticket that was only in English. He is an example of yet another French Canadian who influenced Canada's history by helping restore French as an official language in Manitoba. The question is, did he ever have to pay his parking ticket?

Back to Louis Riel. Born in the Red River colony, he was the oldest of 11 children and was educated in Montréal to become a priest, but Riel eventually made his way back west, where he started working to secure the rights of the

Métis. After leading two rebellions against the Canadian government, Riel was executed in 1885. He had gone kind of crazy, becoming something of a religious fanatic. He came to believe that he had been divinely chosen to represent the Métis community, although maybe he had simply become a bit conceited. He started calling himself Louis "David" Riel, the prophet of a new world, and prayed for days with his arms spread out as if on a cross. Apparently Canadian political power used to have much more effect on people than today.

Another Métis who is often forgotten is Gabriel Dumont, a successful buffalo hunter who created a government based on the structure of a hunter community, the commune of Saint-Laurent. He fought alongside Louis Riel and honed his skills as a guerilla fighter. Once Riel had surrendered, however, Dumont fled to the United States and joined Buffalo Bill's Wild West show. While in the States, Dumont met with several members of French Canadian communities, who had by then heard of the Riel rebellion and associated the Métis plight with their own. Dumont was asked to speak in Montréal by the Société Saint-Jean Baptiste, a nationalist organization. But apparently the tour was a dismal failure because people assumed that Dumont would be as good and diplomatic a speaker as Riel, which he definitely was not. Indeed, one of the first speeches

he delivered criticized the Church for not helping with the rebellion and blaming its representatives for its failure. Of course, in the
1880s, this was not a discourse that was
allowed in Québec, so Dumont's tour was can-
celled, and he was sent back to the States.

Nevertheless, Dumont is a great example of
the journeys inland of French travellers, as his
grandfather was something of a *coureur des
bois*. Dumont's way of life was that of a typical
buffalo hunter. He was recognized for his courage and prowess, and those qualities got him
to where he was; you need more than this
today to get anywhere. He left instructions to
be buried standing up, so the legend says, so
that he could see the river forever, though some
have said he actually wanted to be able to see
the enemy sooner. Or perhaps he simply
wanted to make things more complicated for
the people who had to bury him.

In 1987, Léo Piquette, a Franco-Albertan
politician, made the news when he tried twice
to ask a question in French in the legislative
assembly of Alberta and was interrupted both
times by the Speaker, who stated that Piquette
was not allowed to use French. Piquette argued
back that the Northwest Territories Act (NTA)
actually allowed him to do so and that this act,
although replaced by the Constitution when
Alberta joined Confederation, had never been
repealed. Back in 1905, the act that created

Alberta and Saskatchewan did encompass the NTA, which in essence allowed French to be taught in school. This sparked a provincewide debate, and Francophones throughout the region expressed support for Piquette. In the end, Alberta ruled that people would be allowed to speak French in the assembly, provided that they gave a translation of their questions or speech to the Speaker in advance. One man sparked a huge language debate and forced the province and the country to rethink the validity of their laws. In the end, this was, in the late 1980s, a long overdue victory.

In Saskatchewan, the province revised its founding act (the Manitoba Act of 1870) in the early 20th century, and by 1934, Francophones were allowed only one hour of French instruction per day. The province modified the act in the 1960s and finally granted management of French schools to Francophones.

The debate is not over, however. In 2008, the province of Alberta appealed a court decision to throw out a speeding ticket for a French trucker because a) the ticket was written only in English and b) the speeder, Guy Caron, could not get a hearing in French. However, it was emphasized that some tickets given in Québec are written only in French.

Originally from St. Boniface, the writer Gabrielle Roy, the author of the famous novel

Bonheur d'occasion (The Tin Flute), is considered one of the most important French Canadian writers in Canadian history. She attended French schools and became a teacher in the rural communities that surround Winnipeg. She married another St. Boniface resident, and after spending time in France, she and her husband eventually moved to Montréal, where she began her career as a writer. We can find a quotation from her on our $20 bill: *Nous connaîtrions nous seulement un peu nous-mêmes, sans les arts!* (Would we know ourselves even a little without the arts!). Her novel is an important book that is often required reading in Québec in literature or history classes.

Bonheur d'occasion was one of the first novels of its kind in Canada. Prior to that, novels concentrated on promoting agricultural ideals. These were called *romans du terroir* (novels of the land) and portrayed a polished image of what farm life was like in Québec. It should be noted that when these were written, between 1846 and 1945, Québec was going towards, and living in, its *Grande Noirceur* period. It was during this period that Québec Premier Maurice Duplessis promoted the idea of *la survivance*, essentially that rural life was the solution to survival. These *romans du terroir* promoted just that. But by 1945, agriculture in Québec had changed and people were moving into the cities, so reading about farm life had become less interesting. Gabrielle Roy was one of the first to acknowledge the change and published a novel that would set the tone for the next few years, the urban novel. She has won many prizes such as the Femina award in France, the Governor General's award (three times) and was made a Companion of the Order of Canada. She has since become a prize herself—the Association des littératures canadienne et québécoise offers two annual Gabrielle Roy prizes, one each to an English and a French literary critic.

In Alberta, French radio is what gave power to the community. It was, again, ordinary citizens who fought to increase French broadcasts from seven minutes a day to seven hours a week. The creation in 1949 of a French-only radio station, CHFA, was a huge victory after years of difficult negotiations. One of the Franco-Albertans responsible for the existence of the radio station was Louis Beauchemin, an eminent doctor born in Montréal. After bothering Radio-Canada for many years so that the broadcaster would open a French station in Alberta, Beauchemin figured he was better off doing things himself. He created a private radio station, Radio Edmonton, and started broadcasting. Radio-Canada finally woke up and realized that there were a lot of French Canadians in Alberta who wanted to listen to French radio. It seems the radio executives back then were not too quick to see potential markets.

This advance had significant ramifications because it was a way for French Canadian artists, politicians and others to make their voices heard and to reach a good portion of the population. Just like any other radio station, CHFA had to fund itself by selling advertising airtime. It was difficult to convince businesses that an ad on a French radio station, and a privately owned one on top of that, could reap profits, but the station's management had a good idea. Announcers encouraged listeners to patronize the businesses that advertised on the station and tell them that they had heard their ad on the French station. French solidarity kicked in because it was presented that if listeners wanted their station to survive, they had to do their part. Apparently, the campaign was a huge success and allowed the station to survive for 25 years. CHFA was sold to Radio-Canada in 1974. Before the sale, CHFA only broadcast in Edmonton, but the 1970s saw the expansion of the radio network in Alberta to Lethbridge, Calgary, Red Deer, Peace River, Fort McMurray and other communities. The network was renamed *Première Chaîne* in 1997.

The Prairies are mostly English, no doubt about it. But since they were French at first, how does a language, and a people, become secondary? Although the Canadian Pacific Railway is presented as the real creator of Canada because it physically linked the country together, it wasn't much help to the French in the West. Once the Prairies were connected to the rest of Canada, countless immigrants from everywhere started coming in, and the language they spoke, or decided to learn, was English. The train opened up the West to the world, and this made the French just another nationality in the region. Saskatchewan, for example, has a great number of French community centres, associations, folkdance companies, artists' associations and so on. A few French celebrations are organized every year such as the Fête fransaskoise, held annually in Moose Jaw since the 1980s. The fact that this celebration is funded partly by the Government of Canada through its Canadian Heritage program demonstrates the willingness of the Canadian government to promote bilingualism everywhere.

CHAPTER TWELVE

THE FRENCH JOIE DE VIVRE

It has often been said that French Canadians like to celebrate...a lot. Their taste for parties and get-togethers is called the French *joie de vivre*, which means literally "happy to be alive." The propensity to celebrate, which might sometimes border on carelessness, comes from the *coureur des bois* attitude. As mentioned before, the *coureurs des bois* chose not only a job, but a way of life. This way of life had more freedom than being a settler; men lived in the woods, worked when they wanted or needed to and returned to society once in a while to stock up on money or supplies. The *coureurs* took on some of the habits of the Natives, for example, giving up their religious practice to get more time to...celebrate.

Since the *coureurs* roamed the woods through-out the country, people everywhere in Canada came to see for themselves how carefree and fun the life of the *coureurs* was, and it became sort of idealized into this *joie de vivre* idea. When I say idealized, I mean that this "perfect" life was an illusion because the life of a *coureur* wasn't so rosy. They were cold, hungry, afraid and unsure most of the time. In any case, it is to them that *joie de vivre* came to be linked, and it remains a kind of cliché that French Canadians are a bit crazier than the rest of Canada. We eat more, we drink more, and we celebrate more.

The French imported institutions from home to entertain themselves. An invention of the French, the first cabaret, *Le Chat Noir* (The Black Cat), opened in Paris in 1881. It was a place where local artists could try out their acts in front of other artists. The best-known cabaret was undoubtedly the *Moulin Rouge*, built in 1889 close to Paris. Cabarets were extremely popular right from the start because people could go there and relax. Theatres were a somewhat snobbish venue, and clients were expected to dress up and behave. In the cabarets, patrons could do whatever they felt like doing. This was a groundbreaking idea because before that, people were not allowed to perform, dance or wear costumes except in theatres.

Canadian history books usually trace the first cabaret opening to the 17th century, which would actually make Canada the first country to have a cabaret. The first two cabarets were the *Cabaret de la Folle Ville* (The Crazy Town Cabaret) in Montréal and the *Cabaret de la Saint-Michel* (Cabaret St. Michael) in Lachine.

The French didn't lose any time starting up a nightlife in the New World. There were Royal Ordinances regulating cabarets as early as 1720, meaning that these nightclubs, and the behaviour attached to them, were already bothering some people. It was mostly the sale of alcohol in these establishments that was a problem and not the entertainment, which some may have considered immoral. The government wanted to levy taxes on alcohol so not just anyone could sell it—cabarets required a permit to allow them to get their patrons inebriated. Other restrictions quickly followed, one of which was that cabarets could not serve alcohol later than 10:00 PM, an early closing time by today's standards. New France also tried to restrict how far cabarets could be located outside city walls. Apparently, if cabarets were too far from the city limits, soldiers would show up late for work or leave work early because they had to go too far to drink. By the mid-1700s, there were some 28 cabarets close to Louisbourg on Cape Breton Island, though when governors corresponded with the French government overseas, they reduced the numbers to make it look like we were...not French Canadians. Primarily because the male settlers were bored and there were definitely not enough female partners to make life interesting, these places allowed for the famous French *joie de vivre* to be expressed despite the difficult colony life.

Cabarets, places where singing, drinking and playing games were the main activities, still exist. A bit updated, modern cabarets usually include singing, dancing and drinking, but games have been relegated to other establishments, and women are now allowed in. The development of cabarets was given a boost in 1920 when the U.S. government added an amendment to their Constitution called the Prohibition Act. The act prohibited the sale and import of alcoholic beverages with more than 0.5 percent alcohol. The response of the Québec government was to go the opposite way and create the Liquor Commission in 1921, thereby legalizing and centralizing the sale of alcohol. Montréal became a safe haven not only for American cabaret performers who lost their jobs because of Prohibition, but also for any beer drinker on the continent. So Montréal became the "in" place for Americans to go, as they were forced to sober up in their own country. When the Prohibition Act was repealed in 1933 and Americans were allowed to have booze again, they stopped coming to Canada.

Nevertheless, the boom of the 1920s brought Montréal nightlife, well, to life, and cabarets transformed Montréal into a little Broadway in the 1930s and 1940s. The venue *Cabaret Frolics*, which hosted Texas Guinan, a New York star, on its opening night in 1930, really inaugurated the cabaret period in Montréal. More than 40 cabarets were in operation around Boulevard St. Laurent (nicknamed "the Main") during the 1940s. Many French cabarets still survive today, albeit in different forms. The Monument-National, which now hosts the Festival Juste pour rire, opened in 1893. In 1947, the opening of *Au faisan doré* (The Golden Pheasant) marked an important change in cabaret life, as it was the first Francophone establishment, meaning that not only could people be served in French, but only French artists performed there.

The French *joie de vivre* unfortunately resulted in corruption as well as creating a red-light district out of our Main. This period was a dark one for the city, with crime levels higher than they had ever been. It was assumed that cabarets were somehow linked to the Montréal mafia, and some of them were. This assumption prompted the creation of the Comité de moralité publique (Public Morality Committee), which pushed for investigations of establishments such as cabarets, brothels and game rooms. The committee and the Montréal police cleaned up the streets, but even today, the area has a reputation for being somewhat racy. Places to socialize, drink and celebrate were some of the first cultural imports of the French, so I suppose the idea that the French epitomize the idea of *joie de vivre* is not that far-fetched.

Another typical form of French entertainment in early Canada, the *soirées canadiennes*, were inspired by the family evenings in France—cabaret sort of fun, but at home. In France, family and friends would meet at the stable, which would allow the hosts to keep working while the dancing was going on. In Canada, families would get together in the house, no work was allowed, and everyone would sing and dance all night long (even though dancing was frowned upon by the Church). These *soirées* came to Canada a bit later than the cabarets, however, for the obvious reason that there were not many families at the beginning of the colony.

A time of the year when people usually unite and forget their differences, Christmas was actually a divisive time in early Canada. French Canadians celebrated *Saint-Sylvestre* (New Year's Eve) and the *Jour de l'an* (New Year's Day) as their main holidays. Although Christmas was celebrated, the *Jour de l'an* was really the time for drinking, dancing and, occasionally, shenanigans. At the beginning of New France, New Year's celebrations included a now-vanished tradition called "mumming." This meant that people would go around the village, knocking on doors and barging into people's homes, usually making fools of themselves by singing, dancing, joking or perhaps stumbling around (if alcohol was in the mix). Mumming was originally a Christmas tradition in Britain, with groups of people going from house to house presenting a play to raise money. But, of course, French Canadians added a little spice to the concept.

For a long time, Christmas was the English holiday, while New Year's was mostly celebrated by the French. Actually, if we think that the French created the idea of *joie de vivre*, it should be no surprise that they celebrated both holidays—two occasions to get together and have a family party. The French Canadian *Jour de l'an* was seen as a secular celebration and a night for debauchery, according to the English bourgeoisie. What changed the situation was (surprise, surprise) the Church. It did not approve of New Year's and wanted the focus to be on Christmas as a religious holiday. An effort was made to make the day more religious and also more centred on children. Now, there is no question that Christmas is for children, but French Canadians have made the New

Year's party an important celebration throughout the country. After all, we plan our New
Year's Eve celebrations almost as carefully as
our Christmas dinner.

CHAPTER THIRTEEN

FRENCH CANADIAN ARTS AND LETTERS

French theatre was a notable and early import to the New World. As early as 1606, a piece written by Marc Lescarbot titled *Le théâtre de Neptune* was produced and presented to a small crowd in New France (small not because of a lack of interest, but rather a lack of people). This entertainment might have been the first of its kind in North America, but we know for sure it was definitely the first in Canada. Both Frenchmen and Natives played characters in the piece, and it was recited in barges close to the shore. Written as a welcome back to Champlain on his return from months of exploration inland, it included singing, trumpet playing and several little scenes, of which the texts have survived, but not the music. Here is a short passage from this first piece of Canadian theatre, accompanied by my humble translation:

> Va heureusement et poursuis ton chemin
> Ou le sort te conduit : car je voy le destin
> Préparer à la France un Florissant empire
>
> Vive Henry le grand roy des François
> Qui fait maintenant vivre souz ses loys
> Les nations de sa Nouvelle-France

English translation:

> Go on happily and follow your way
> Where fate leads you because
>   I see destiny
> Preparing for France a flourishing empire
>
> Hail to Henry, the great king of the French
> Who now has living under his laws
> The nations of his New France

Lescarbot has gone down in our books as the first theatrical producer, but his career was much more than acting offshore in a canoe. He wrote *Histoire de la Nouvelle France* (History of New France), partly witnessed and partly invented, which recorded some of the early events that would have otherwise been lost to history. His later versions differed from the first in that he became increasingly more present and more active as the versions evolved. He enjoyed visiting the tribes living near the colony and noted very carefully how they behaved, what they did and how they acted with each other. In a way, he was treating them better than say, Champlain or others who had different agendas. He was fascinated by the Natives and devoted a large part of his *History* to them. The fact that they were asked to take part in his *Théâtre de Neptune* could be seen as another way in which he showed them respect.

French theatre was just in its beginnings when New France was founded. King Louis XIII had created the Académie française in 1635, an institution for the development of the arts. Lescarbot was undoubtedly influenced by the three main writers of that time, Pierre Corneille, Jean Racine and Molière. All three were considered classic playwrights in that they wrote tragic theatre. In essence, a tragedy is a heroic story of hardship and difficult choices. Lescarbot's *Neptune* was somewhat written along these lines. The story was about a group of mythical figures, including Neptune, the god of the sea, who got together to welcome travellers who had been on a long voyage and were returning home.

The next recorded play was written in honour of the coming to power of Louis XIV. Charles

Montmagny, then governor of New France, organized a piece in which demons chased a non-Christian soul and ended up catching it and bringing it with them to Hell. A peculiar element figured in this play—the demons spoke Algonquin. Montmagny apparently wanted the Natives attending the play to understand something of what was going on, though it does seem odd that the Native language was used as a demonic tongue in a primarily religious play. Perhaps the message was subliminal; either way, it wasn't exactly a discreet criticism of the Natives' way of life. What this event seems to suggest is that plays were only organized to celebrate something else. Going to see a play just to see a play was not something that early French Canadians did. Rather, they would watch a performance as part of a larger celebration or were even required to attend such an event to show their patriotism for France, the motherland. In any case, the fact that plays were organized as part of celebrations means that they were a relatively popular form of culture and a way to remember home. Indeed, the great majority of plays performed in the early years of the nation were not original pieces but well-known French and English works.

Theatre was also a way to patch things up between the conquered and the conqueror. In the late 18th century, English soldiers performed a couple of plays completely in the French language, which was certainly appreciated by French Canadians. Perhaps this was not only to be "nice"—the French Canadians were still the main population in Canada, so they were the only audience a play could get. Pleasing the French Canadians was a necessity as much as a peaceful gesture. Following the Conquest, theatre became increasingly English, and French audiences slowly started to pull away, en masse after the *Patriotes* rebellions. Many theatrical establishments, called playrooms, opened following the Conquest, but they offered entertainment in English only. I suppose it was okay until French Canadians became embittered by the inequality between the two cultures. Plus, they must have grown tired of always seeing the same Shakespeare plays.

To counter the trend towards English dominance of the theatre, Joseph Quesnel, a French Canadian, worked to preserve French culture, which was in danger of being lost if people stopped encouraging local artists. In 1780, Quesnel founded a theatre company called *Les jeunes messieurs canadiens* in Montréal to try to muster up some interest in French Canadian theatre. The company performed plays by Molière and others, and disbanded close to 30 years after its inception. They also performed in what is considered the first Canadian opera, composed by Quesnel himself, called *Colas et Colinette*, the story of two French Canadian peasants whose love is challenged by a bailiff who wants Colinette for himself.

Quesnel was an interesting character. He was taken prisoner by the British while on a ship that was bringing ammunition and weapons to the American colonies during the revolution. His punishment was to remain in British North America until the end of the hostilities. While he was stuck in Canada, he started his theatre company, an action that didn't go over well with the Church. Shortly before the company's first performance, the parish priest gave a sermon that demonized theatrical events. According to the priest, theatre was a devious form of entertainment that kept people away from the Church, and he stated that absolution would be refused to anyone attending Quesnel's plays. In a way, then, Quesnel was a rebel throughout his life, first by trying to help the revolution in the American colonies, and then by making theatre somewhat edgy. It wasn't hard to be a rebel back then—a simple play was enough to anger the authorities, in this case, the Church. Quesnel's theatre troupe worked hard to preserve French Canadian culture, and the influence of its members on society went beyond the stage because most of them had day jobs as lawyers, politicians or other "regular" employment.

The Catholic Church really didn't approve of the theatre, and wherever it had enough power, it tried to stop theatre development. In Montréal, for example, it was forbidden to stage plays on Sundays, a day that was supposed to be dedicated to God, not to foolish entertainment. The Church was powerful enough to get the law accepted and respected (or was it?) and even ruled the schedules of its believers. The city also charged an amusement tax on ticket sales, which kept people out of the theatres because it was too expensive. In the end, the restrictive attitude of the Church in Montréal helped the city in one indirect way—there were no more travelling performing troupes, so local actors had more opportunities to be discovered and make a career out of reciting someone else's words.

The works of well-known playwrights Corneille, who wrote *Le Cid*, and Molière, who wrote *Tartuffe*, are still performed in French theatres in each province. Each one of the Prairie Provinces has its own French theatre—Le Cercle Molière in Winnipeg, La Troupe du Jour in Saskatoon and L'Unithéâtre in Edmonton. Even BC has a venue called Théâtre la Seizième in Vancouver. The name of this theatre has an interesting story.

When Théâtre la Seizième opened in the 1970s, it produced a piece written by a then-emerging French Canadian writer, Michel

Tremblay. His play was called *Les Belles Soeurs* (The Sisters-in-Law) in which he presented the lives of 15 women. The Vancouver theatre company was headed by a woman, whom her team called the 16th woman of the play, *la seizième*. This is a great demonstration of the nation-wide collaboration between French Canadians—a theatre in Vancouver bears a name inspired by a French Canadian Montréaler. The Winnipeg theatre, opened in 1925, is said to be the oldest theatre company in Canada. Le Cercle innovated by producing pieces written by French Canadians, Michel Tremblay included, instead of the classic Shakespeare or Molière. Continuing interest in this theatre company was confirmed recently when it was awarded $1.6 million by the provincial and federal governments to build a new performance venue at a total cost of $5 million.

Along with theatre, the printed word was another art form that got an early start in New France. Shortly after the Conquest, a Frenchman from Lyon, Fleury Mesplet, began producing a newspaper. He can also be credited for opening the first printing facility, as well as being the first printer in Canada. It is true that prior to that, French Canadian culture was remembered through oral history but not recorded per se. New France had been discovered through manual engravings and books printed in Europe, which sometimes made their way back to the New World. Fleury Mesplet had been arrested for sedition and forced to give up a primary paper, *La Gazette de Québec*, because of its strong annexation stance. Annexation in this case meant the wish to secede from Canada and become part of the United States. This was a relatively popular movement at the time because many French Canadians thought that perhaps they had more in common with the Americans than the British. The fact that France had helped the American colonies during the revolution might have cemented this belief. In any case, Mesplet was not an exception, but his writings certainly made the British angry. Upon his return from incarceration in 1785, Mesplet started to produce *La Gazette de Montréal*, a Francophone paper and one of the first newspapers in Canada. *The Halifax Gazette* of 1752 and *La Gazette de Québec* of 1764 (the pro-annexation one) both lay claim to being the oldest, period. Mesplet's *Gazette de Québec* might not have been the first Canadian newspaper, but it is the oldest continuously published newspaper still in print today, an impressive feat considering all the historical events that have caused most newspapers to fold at one point or another. *La Gazette de Montréal* was eventually published as a French and English newspaper to get as much readership as it could. Finally, it ended up as *The Montréal*

Gazette, the only English newspaper available in Montréal. The one Anglophone source of information in Montréal, then, owes its existence to a Frenchman. There is a park in the Old Port of Montréal that bears Mesplet's name, and an annual book trade show in the city that awards the Prix Fleury-Mesplet every year to an individual who has actively worked in the promotion of editing in Québec. This is to encourage French Canadians to continue the centuries-old work of Mesplet to produce original French Canadian printed work.

In Ontario, printing developed much later, but it grew quickly. In the 19th century, some 40 French newspapers started up, 30 of which operated only in Ottawa. This might have been in response to the waves of Québecois immigrating to the area. It also made Ottawa the French Canadian capital of Ontario, which it still is today, having the largest French population outside Québec. Franco-Ontarians came later to the printing world, but they caught up pretty fast.

Until the rebellions of 1837–38, not much was accomplished in French Canadian literature besides acquiring books written overseas. Before that, literature consisted mostly of travel journals and informative books about Canada written by Frenchmen who usually elected not to live here. If we count these as literary works, then surely Cartier is our first writer, because he talked about the land in his journal. A book was "discovered" and said to have been written around 1790, which would make it the first book about the area we now call Ontario. The book's author signed only his initials, JCB, so to this day, we have no clue who wrote it, exactly what time period it refers to or when it was published. It is a literary mystery that has never been solved. Breathtaking. But if we think in terms of original writing, perhaps more fiction than information, we have to wait until 1837 for the first novel. This first French Canadian novel, written by Philippe Aubert de Gaspé, was called *L'influence d'un livre* (The Influence of a Book), which was about the lack of spiritual life in French Canada. The book in the title was, of course, the Bible. For a long while, literary works were supposed to present a moral and pious image, and rare were those that went against this idea. De Gaspé's book was considered too satirical and talked a bit too much about superstitious beliefs. Until the 1960s, a version that had been modified by a priest circulated, until the censored parts were eventually found and inserted back into the novel. Nothing crazy, no nudity or sacrilegious material; simply the description of certain common superstitions and other uneventful chapters, which makes you wonder how sensitive the censoring priest was. Eventually, as society secularized, writing also secularized and started to present more realistic stories—and the Church stopped censoring books as well.

In 1877, French Canadian writers met at what was the first literary convention in Canada. In honour of the 25th anniversary of the Institut canadien-français, attendees at the meeting decided what actions they would take to protect French culture in Ontario. For example, the writers in attendance wanted to open public libraries, hold annual literary events, provide free language courses (in French, I assume; if not, that would ruin the purpose, wouldn't it?) and increase the distribution of Canadian works in schools (again, I assume French Canadian works). There was an Institut canadien both in Montréal and in Ottawa, and they sought to do the same thing—promote French Canadian culture, which sometimes meant being at odds with the Catholic Church (surprise, surprise). The convention took place in Ottawa and was organized by Joseph Tassé, a writer, parliamentarian and translator. This convention was a way for Tassé to get French Canadian writers from Ontario and Québec to mingle and discover each other's work. It was perhaps also a way to cement the link between the two similar yet different cultures and to remind Québeckers that they were not alone. Of course, the gathering took place because the Church had no objections to it, but the Governor General had also encouraged the project.

Among the writers emerging in Ottawa and attending the convention, notice must be made of Benjamin Sulte, probably one of Canada's first historians. Sulte's greatest work was a history of French Canadians, from their beginnings as a nation to the present. "The present" back then was something like 1880, so Sulte only had to cover 200 years...which he did in some six volumes. The edition I have read was perhaps double the size of a regular book, which makes his work even longer. Sulte broke new ground by looking at the way of life of "regular" people instead of focusing only on great men. Thanks to him, we have a pretty good idea of what people ate every day, the clothes they wore, how they spoke and what they thought...or at least what Sulte thought people should think. This approach also meant he was rather critical of the religious institutions. Talking about the daily life of people showed how present and perhaps invasive the Church was. This, of course, got him into trouble, but he defended every word of his massive study. He was rather direct and opinionated, and some of his detractors got mad enough to call him a traitor because he was perceived as criticizing the glory of France and its men. I have read the numerous volumes of his history, and I thought he treated everyone well, seeing bravery and courage in actions that today we'd probably find stupid and pointless. Let's just say he really thought French Canadians were the greatest people on earth. To say he was a prolific author is an understatement. An inventory of his articles and books ranges close to 3000, and there are certainly some works missing. But writing so much almost necessarily means that Sulte sometimes wrote about trivial things. For example, he wrote an ode to the Canada goose, a four-page essay on how to prepare the bird. He ended an excruciating listing of ingredients and instructions with this statement:

> If my discourse to you seems more supple than before, it is only because I have taken a bite of that stuffing I was just describing. Long live the Canadian goose!

So, it's probably better to remember Sulte for his history of the French Canadians than his recipes.

An early French Canadian writer, Émile Nelligan, was a poet whose life was perhaps even more dramatic than his writings. His poems were highly religious and many of them talked about death, like this one. Again, this is my humble translation, which can only tell you what he is trying to say but in no way as beautifully as he does:

Comme il est douloureux de voir un
  corbillard,
Traîné par des chevaux funèbres, en
  automne,
S'en aller cahotant au chemin monotone,
Là-bas vers quelques gris cimetière perdu,
Qui lui-même comme un grand mort
  gît étendu!

English translation:

It is so painful to see a hearse
Pulled by funerary horses, in the fall
Jolting along the monotonous road
Over there, towards a forgotten
  grey cemetery
Which lies there as a tall corpse would.

Nelligan had a nervous breakdown early on in his life and remained affected until his death. In fact, he was institutionalized for the last 25 years of his life, and during that time, he endlessly rewrote his existing poems from memory. We know that he was inspired by Charles Beaudelaire, because he wrote a poem about him. This admiration might have contributed to putting him over the edge—Beaudelaire was an "interesting" character to say the least. A rebel, Beaudelaire dyed his hair blue, used laudanum unashamedly and dated prostitutes openly. He spent the last days of his life paralyzed from the long-term use of laudanum and died completely broke and not really recognized. Nelligan had started his career early, publishing poems at only 16 years of age, but he was never really recognized during his lifetime, either. His mental health had always been fragile, so he simply never recovered from his breakdown, and perhaps the lack of recognition. Unlike Beaudelaire, his condition was not self-inflicted, which makes his story even more dramatic. Just like many other artists throughout history, Nelligan became famous only after his death.

A modern French Canadian writer who has greatly influenced Canadian literature is Michel Tremblay from Québec. Tremblay has broken all barriers during his career, making French Canadian slang (called *joual*) into a literary language and talking about subjects that were considered taboo by the Church, even in the 20th century. These subjects are not so shocking by today's standards, but some 40 years ago, talking about the working class, for example, was something that had not been done before. His first piece, written in 1965, was titled *Les Belles-Soeurs*. The play is about a woman who wins a million sticky stamps, exchangeable for furniture. She needs to stick the stamps into booklets, so she calls her friends, 14 of them, to come and help her. The action in the play stems from the conversation of the women—and having an all-woman cast was yet another first that Tremblay could call his own. The play features working-class women complaining about their lives, something that happened but was certainly never talked about in public. In theory, women were happy the way they were—the Church said so. So when the following lines appeared in Tremblay's *Les Belles-Soeurs*, it caught the attention of Québec society as a whole:

> ...Then I work. I work like a demon.
> I don't stop 'til noon. I wash...Dresses,
> shirts, stockings, sweaters, underpants,
> bras. The works. I scrub it, wring it out,
> scrub it again, rinse it. My hands are
> chapped, my back is sore. I curse like
> hell.

Tremblay's books were groundbreaking because not only were they written in "slang," but they referred to specific streets in Montréal, which made his stories believable. His characters have now become part of Québec culture, *Les Belles-Soeurs* being a good example, just like Evangeline had been in Nova Scotia. His characters were featured in more than one work, so readers got to know another side of a character they had met in a different story. Tremblay developed an imaginary group of people who became well known to most Québeckers. The author made the working class "cool." It was the first time that lower French

Canadian classes were treated as literary subjects, and it worked. It worked so well, in fact, that his plays have been translated into numerous languages. The struggles that his working-class characters dealt with were the same throughout the world—the lack of social mobility, relationship and family problems and lack of money, among others. He also wrote many plays with homosexual characters, which crossed yet another bridge in Canadian literature. Tremblay has always been a separatist—he refused the Order of Canada in 1990 out of principle. But his work is as popular in English as in French. After all, the struggles were and are the same whether you speak English or French.

Antonine Maillet figures at the top of the list of influential French Canadian writers, if only for bringing Acadian culture to the forefront of Canadian culture. She is the author of a novel, published in 1971, depicting a washerwoman called La Sagouine. She did the same for Acadia that Tremblay has done for Québec—each used the language of the people and the region in their work. *La Sagouine*, one of Maillet's most popular works, is written entirely in Chiac, a dialect of Acadian French mixed with English. Here is La Sagouine speaking about the war, in a translated version of the language:

Between 'n the war, they was an idle period where not'n was happenin no more. Not'n was happenin in'em days 'n we could of very well croaked like stray animals in their holes. But they was the war. Got here jus' in time, it did. Just in the nick of time to save us fr'm poverty.

Maillet wrote countless stories, all based in Acadia, and many of the characters that she created have become symbols, which means that people identify with her work. Besides Maillet and Tremblay, there are numerous other French Canadian writers who have had just as much influence in French Canadian literature.

French Canadians have been as prolific with singing words as writing them. French Canadian music takes on many influences, but it originally featured the Irish fiddle as a main instrument. The French folk songs that have been sung for years in Canada are the same ones that ignited parties back in France. The French repertoire was brought to the New World, but it was enlarged and modified with some local flavour. Our *coureurs des bois* and *voyageurs* sang the old French songs as they paddled away from civilized society, the beat of the song guiding the rhythm of the paddles and the speed of the canoe. In the 1800s, several French Canadians tried to make an

inventory of the folk songs of Canada and realized they were the same as those in France. In
France, the words changed according to the
province you were in, and the same happened
in Canada. In 1865, a compendium of folk
songs was published that traced the origins of
two songs, "Bal chez Boulé" and "Vive la Canadienne," the first songs to be imported and
performed here. The first song tells the tale of
a man who danced so badly he was ejected
from the ball he was invited to, while the latter
song is considered the first patriotic French
Canadian song. Although the origins of some
songs are questionable, it is undeniable that
the music and the words came directly from the
French repertoire.

The first, and perhaps the best-known French
Canadian folksinger was Marie-Rose-Anne
Bolduc, called La Bolduc. She sang traditional
songs at the Monument-National, a popular
cabaret of the 1930s in Montréal. Although her
songs were usually lively and relatively happy,
she'd had to struggle with several issues for
most of her life. She lost eight children when
they were at a young age, and she ended her
life battling cancer and her insurance company. In 1937, she was in a bad car accident,
and a head injury caused memory loss and an
inability to concentrate, which in essence
ended her singing career. While she was recu-
perating, she was diagnosed with cancer. Her

insurance refused to pay her anything, and she ended up spending her own money on cancer treatments. Not only was she the first French Canadian singer-songwriter, but she was also a career woman when most women were housewives, by choice or not. Women in the public sphere were a rare thing and were not looked upon positively. La Bolduc did not have to fight a bad reputation, since she was, after all, a respectable married woman, taking her husband to some of her gigs and using her married name as her artist name: Madame Édouard Bolduc. She was a true success story—she and her husband were relatively poor, she had no formal training of any kind, and yet she became a star and was considered the queen of the *chansonniers* in Québec.

French Canadian music has evolved into diverse styles, and some of them have gained international recognition. The best-known artist is undoubtedly Celine Dion, probably one of the most widely recognized singers in the world. I did have some qualms about whether or not to talk about her in this book, mostly because I don't listen to her music, so I don't connect with the fact that she has such a huge following. Nevertheless, Dion did put Canada on the world map, and she is faithful to her roots, speaking French as often as possible, even in English performances. She made the news in Québec when she refused a prize because it celebrated her as an Anglophone artist. On live TV, she said she could not accept such an award because she was Francophone, despite the fact that she sang in English. If this is not staying true to your roots, I don't know what is. Dion often underlines how simple a life she lives, although I wonder how simple it really is. She made a successful switch to singing in English, reaching the American market, a feat that seems to be difficult to achieve even for English-speaking Canadian artists. Her name was on everyone's lips once she sang the theme song for one of the highest grossing movies of all time, *Titanic*, and she has not stopped since then. She had a long-standing show in Las Vegas, and she performed on the Plains of Abraham for Québec City's 400th anniversary.

Daniel Lavoie is a notable Manitoba artist who has been singing for close to 40 years. Born in St. Boniface in 1949, his real name was Gerald, which he decided to change to a name that didn't make it sound as if he was 60 years old. He learned to play music from the Jesuits, a religious order that has been able to evolve with the times and do more than just go around converting people. Probably the best-known Franco-Manitoban, Lavoie's career spans decades and has crossed many bridges. He is well known in France, having been honoured in Cannes, and he has also managed to get his name recognized by Americans. He was featured on a show with Liza Minelli, and his music was played on the soap opera *General Hospital*. The decadent Cannes festival, the peculiar Liza and soapy love stories—Lavoie can really do everything.

From the Maritimes, there is one person who comes to mind immediately, Edith Butler, a woman who has made a name for herself and for the Acadians. She started her career in Moncton, singing to pay for her education. Soon she was touring Québec and France, winning prize after prize for the song that made her famous, "De Paquetville." If we talk about Acadian music, the most popular musician is probably Zachary Richard, an Acadian from Louisiana who has made a career singing in French, mixing with it the Cajun-style music that has made Louisiana famous.

If we stay on the topic of music and perhaps a bit more in my generation, Simple Plan is definitely a group we should discuss. Formed by five French Canadians from Montréal, the pop punk group has toured the world many times and produced two albums that have sold a total of seven million copies. They often come back to Canada, and they usually offer, on top of performances in big commercial venues, surprisingly intimate shows for only a few hundred fans, demonstrating that they, too, remain conscious of their roots. Their name supposedly comes from a plan they actually formulated. They were mildly successful as a punk bank in Montréal and decided on a simple plan— to "sell out" and become world famous. Simple, but brilliant.

From a simple plan to French Canadian painting. Apparently, Canadians figured in French paintings as early as 1550. But these works were not created by people who actually went to the New World. Painters simply imagined what Canada looked like, based on the writings of travellers who had visited the colonies, which certainly made for inaccurate depictions of the landscape. If we consider maps to be paintings, then Samuel de Champlain was an accomplished artist, drawing somewhat accurately the contours of the area he had just discovered. In a similar manner, as early as 1685, there were small drawings and paintings circulating that depicted the fauna and flora of the new territory—perhaps it was useful to know what kinds of things existed in the New World, but sometimes the quality of the drawings made them worthy to be called "art." While depictions of the New World circulated in France, the opposite took place here, with settlers bringing French paintings with them or, at least, bringing their memory of what the currently popular painting of the period was. When discussing early painting in Canada, then, we are talking mainly about a continuation of the artistic movement in France, at least at the beginning of the colony.

For the Jesuit priests, French engravings served as tools for conversion. They would use images of religious ceremonies or objects to illustrate what they were trying to teach. In the movie *Amistad*, a slave becomes Christian after looking at pictures of Jesus on the cross and other printed images in a Bible. Whether this was true or not, we don't know, but surely images made life a bit easier for priests trying to explain their deep spiritual beliefs to people who didn't even speak their language. For the most part, though, true Canadian paintings were rare, if only because settlers had other things to do than paint—building shelters, growing food and surviving the winter, for example.

What changed the paintings over the years was simply that the landscape and the people were different in Canada—there are no major turning points to trace back. One family, the Baillairges, was influential in Canada mostly because its members were all artists, and their work spanned five generations. All five generations worked closely either in sculpture, paintings and/or architecture.

Antoine Plamondon was a painter in the 1830s and had such talent that his work was purchased by Lord Durham (the one who said

French Canada had no history) and exhibited in the House of Commons. He taught what he knew to Théophile Hamel, who became an even bigger success story than Plamondon. Hamel became an official portrait painter, meeting political figures of the time and helping them live on through his work.

Mural painting was apparently popular in Canada, as well as mystical painting, both related to Catholicism and demonstrating yet again how present the Church was. Murals were painted mostly between Confederation and the Depression years, beginning with the need to depict a new country and ending when the country had no more money to pay for the paintings. While English Canadian muralists focused on subjects such as patriotism, commercialism and sometimes the Protestant religion, French Canadian painters seem to concentrate on the Catholic religion. This could be explained by the fact that what distinguished the French from the rest of the Confederation was their religion, so it became a way to express their unique identity. Murals were painted mostly in churches, but also in public buildings. The Church usually commissioned the murals (that is, they paid the painter), so the work had to show the religion in a positive light. Between the 1920s and 1940s, painting remained oriented towards religion, perhaps to show how different the

French Canadians were from the rest of the nation or because the Church paid for everything, or perhaps because this period of Depression and pre–World War II was a tough one and people turned to the Church for comfort. Either way, painting in French Canada was "divine" for a long time.

In the 1940s, painting became "edgy," as a group of artists, including painters Jean-Paul Riopelle and Paul-Émile Borduas, published a manifesto called *Le Refus global* (Total Refusal) in which they called for anarchism and the rejection of all societal norms, whether they were in painting, poetry or society in general. At the time, the manifesto was not very popular, but it slowly became a valued piece of work in the context of the Quiet Revolution in Québec. Here are some bits and pieces from the manifesto, enough to give you a sense of how angry these French Canadians were:

> A colony trapped and abandoned as long ago as 1760 beneath unscalable walls of fear (familiar refuge of the vanquished)— its leaders taking to sea or selling themselves to the conqueror, as always when the time is ripe.

> We foresee a future in which man is freed from useless chains, to realize a plenitude of individual gifts, in necessary

unpredictability, spontaneous and resplendent anarchy.

Until then, without surrender or rest, in community of feeling with those who thirst for better life, without fear of setbacks, in encouragement or persecution, we shall pursue in joy our overwhelming need for liberation.

Riopelle had learned his craft under Borduas, and they were both members of a group called Les Automatistes, which meant they painted abstract art, the way it came to them (that is, "automatically"). So the norms that had been observed in art until then went completely against what Borduas and Riopelle wanted to do. Abstract art was miles away from mystical and mural painting—it was open to interpretation, left much to the imagination and rejected any form of logic that had previously been strictly followed. Not an art buff myself, I've always had trouble finding deep meaningful elements when looking at a couple of black squares painted on a white background, but that's why I study history and not art. Both painters were tremendously influential in bringing this movement into Canada and changing the way painters and artists were seen. In fact, they seemed to suggest that artists should be more concerned with their surrounding environment rather than isolating themselves in their art.

Let's now jump into a completely different art form—the circus. A circus is not artistic, you might say, because it has elephants running around and clowns falling into buckets of water. But French Canadian Guy Laliberté contributed to Canadian history by making the country known throughout the world for the Cirque du Soleil, an original and artistic adaptation of the concept of circus. Throughout history, a circus has been a group of travelling performers, usually including clowns, acrobats, loud emcees and perhaps the odd woman with a beard. The Cirque du Soleil travels, but it offers much more than red noses and hairy women. The shows have a coherent storyline, and the performers do things with their bodies that would kill me if I tried them. Back in 1982, the Cirque du Soleil was just a group of street performers walking on stilts and calling themselves "The High Heels Club." I think it's a good thing they decided to modify their act and their name because I don't know how successful a career they would have had. I mean, how long can you walk on stilts? The performers had the great idea to organize a travelling show and add other numbers to their act. In 1984, for the celebration of the 450th anniversary of Cartier's arrival in the St. Lawrence Valley, funding was allocated to Laliberté to create a show commemorating the arrival of the first Europeans in Canada. The show was successful and demands to tour the show came from all over Québec. Years later, the Cirque du Soleil is known internationally and has several permanent shows all over the world, most notably in Las Vegas and soon in Macau. It employs some 4000 employees worldwide, but its base is still in Québec. The confirmation of the Cirque's importance was illustrated in 2007, when they were asked to perform the pre-game show for Superbowl XLI in Miami. What greater accomplishment is there than presenting a show to a stadium full of half-drunk football fans? Actually, it was a pretty good marketing pitch considering the number of (more sober) people watching the game on television. A hotel in Las Vegas has spent some 100 million to build a theatre for the Cirque's *O* show, a circus performance done completely under water. Who would have guessed that looking at a giant aquarium filled with weirdly dressed people could be so interesting?

Canada is known for its many festivals and those are, of course, a direct influence of the French desire to celebrate everything. The word *festival* actually showed up in the French vocabulary in the 1830s and means what it sounds like—a festive celebration. Festivals have been going on for a while, however. We can trace the celebration of festivals back to the ancient Egyptians, who celebrated the changing seasons, for example, getting together at the beginning of harvest time. But if we think of the French *joie de vivre*, it seems only natural to assume there is indeed a little French in all our festivals. Here in Canada, I think it is safe to say that there is a festival for everything, from a potato festival to a snow festival. There is a reggae festival in Alberta, a shellfish festival in PEI, a South Asian film festival in BC, a corn and apple festival in Manitoba, a storytelling festival in Yukon, a bread and honey festival in Ontario, a mascot festival in Québec and a festival of words in Saskatchewan. Needless to say, these are blind picks from a seemingly unending list of Canadian festivals.

Among this list are two world-renowned festivals that take place every year in Montréal, both created by French Canadians. The internationally acclaimed Festival de Jazz de Montréal was started by Alain Simard, a French Canadian who simply wanted people to discover the many talents in the jazz domain. In operation since 1980, the festival gathers some 2.5 million people who come to listen to more than 3000 jazz and blues artists, and it has become the largest music festival in Canada. It is one of the many events that attracts tourists from all over the world. Festivals are legion in

Montréal because there is such a huge tourist market right at our door. Another festival is Juste pour rire (Just for Laughs), which now features shows throughout the nation. An idea of Gilbert Rozon, the comedy celebration was first a French-language-only festival, but seeing as it was also the only comedy festival in the world, the rest of the country followed suit. Juste pour rire has grown into a corporation, producing television shows that are translated into many languages and broadcast throughout the world, even on airplanes. The organization now has offices in Toronto, New York, Los Angeles and other big cities, making the festival a truly international one. The French *joie de vivre* gets us international recognition for being people who like to celebrate everything.

CHAPTER FOURTEEN

FRENCH CANADIAN FOOD AND DRINK

Many of the French settlers who came to Canada were from Normandy, while the rest mostly came from the provinces of Brittany and Picardy. The people who first lived in Normandy were extremely powerful, enough that they actually conquered England in the 11th century, changing the course of English history. Maybe the Conquest of 1760 was only payback for the complete takeover of the English nation by the French in 1066...or perhaps not. The English language is derived from Anglo-Norman, the Old French that was brought to the region. English and French speakers, then, are not so different after all. Our Norman ancestors are responsible for two important imports to Canada: apple orchards and brioche. Normandy is indeed known for its many orchards, its passion for apple cider and its many recipes made with the fruit, such as mussels *à la normande* and tarts. In Canada, we have kept a similar interest in apples, as you can easily find orchards in almost every province. Many Canadian children remember going apple picking with their parents on a cool day in September. It was often part of the ritual of going back to school, sad for the kids, usually not so sad for the parents.

Normandy is also said to be the birthplace of the brioche, an import appreciated by many on weekend mornings. A French bread made with butter, eggs flour and yeast, the name brioche is a deformation of the word *broyer*, which means "to knead." It is often recalled, perhaps wrongly—we will never know—that Marie Antoinette, the wife of Louis XV (the king under whose reign the French Revolution occurred) once said: "Let them eat brioche." While the speaker of this famous line might not have been the Queen of France, the context in which it was said makes sense. At that time in France, a law existed stating that if regular bread was not available, fancier bread (that is, brioche) had to be sold to the public at the same price.

King Louis XV gets the credit for creating another very popular Canadian culinary delight—French onion soup. As history remembers it, the king was hungry one night and only had champagne, butter and onions. He cooked the three together and created the first version of the soup.

Cretons are a well-known French Canadian food that really originated here, but it conspicuously resembles a dish from Normandy, called *rillettes au greton*, a type of pâté made from pork...which is exactly what *cretons* are. In fact, it is pork that has been cooked for so long that all the liquid evaporates, leaving only a paste perfect for spreading on toast. While it might not be considered part of a healthy breakfast, it is part of a traditional French Canadian one.

Another French Canadian specialty based on Norman food is the famous *oreilles de crisses*, which are served at *cabanes à sucre* (sugar shacks). Basically chips made from deep-fried pork jowls, these crunchy morsels were a great source of much-needed fat for the *coureurs des bois* and are now a great source of cholesterol—but also a classic part of sugar shack menus. Some recipes use salt pork as the main ingredient, but traditionally, it should be pork fat, or lard, which ideally would be collected from the cooking of a ham. The fat is then fried in a pan until it is hard enough to have the same consistency, shape and unhealthy cholesterol level as chips. The name *oreilles de crisses* could come either from the word *crisser*, which means "to crackle," as in the sound this food makes in your mouth, or the name is sometimes translated as "Christ's ears"—yet another illustration of how we still include religion in our daily lives, albeit in a somewhat unceremonious manner.

Settlers from Brittany brought Breton crêpes with them, another great addition to the Canadian diet, although the crêpes that the early Canadians served were a much thicker version of the original ones. The Picards who came here brought their knowledge of a product that makes any dessert a success: crème Chantilly. Indeed, the region of Picardy promotes itself as being the home of the sweet delight. We, of course, have adapted it to whipped cream, simply omiting the vanilla.

Another typically French Canadian food, *tarte au sucre* (sugar pie), is actually originally from the Ardennes region of France. *Graisse de rôti*, yet another food imported from France that French Canadians call their own, is made from the fat left over from roasting pork. After slow cooking the pork in water, you bring the leftover fat and water to a boil, then pour it into a bowl and let stand until it becomes hard and ready to slather onto a piece of fresh, crusty bread. Yes, you've got it right, it's a pork-fat spread. Although I am not a big fan, most Québeckers will spend countless hours explaining why one particular recipe or another is so good and so comforting. I haven't been convinced yet—I prefer peanut butter on my toast, not the fat left over from another recipe.

Most of the foods we think of as typically French Canadian usually hark back to an old French recipe. *Boudin noir* (blood pudding or blood sausage), *tourtière* (meat pie) and *porc frais* (roast pork) were all specialty foods back in France but became staple meals here in Canada. In fact, now we go to a sugar shack to enjoy them, or we wait until Christmas because only our grandparents still make that stuff, and the food is not considered fancy at all.

The one meal that we can truly call a French Canadian invention is our famous poutine, which has been poked fun at even by American comedians. If you have been hiding in a cave for, say, 30 years, and you don't know what poutine is, let me explain, while trying to make it sound good (an impossible feat, if you ask me). You take a good portion of French fries, which were called freedom fries for a while in the United States because the French always find a way to make the Americans mad. Next, delicately sprinkle some cheese curds onto the pile of fries. If you like living on the edge (of cardiac arrest), hide some more cheese underneath the fries to double the flavour. Then drown said crunchy fries with a thick, brown gravy that is nearing the solid stage, so as to make the fries soggier than a hot chicken sandwich. Wait a few minutes to make sure the concoction has attained the level of sogginess and cheese meltiness required, and enjoy—ideally with a Pepsi to complete the cliché. To make the dish even more distinguished, some people add smoked meat or replace the gravy with spaghetti sauce. Lovely.

To conclude a classy meal of poutine, a similarly fancy dessert is required. French Canadians from Acadia have created a pastry they call *pets de soeur*, which literally means "nun's farts." I'm sure this fixation with religious connotations in swearing and cooking could be studied in depth, and some weird character peculiarities would be uncovered. In any case, the recipe for *pets de soeur* is pretty simple, probably created to use up any remaining pie crust dough left over after a day of cooking. It is simply pie dough slathered with (of course) butter, cinnamon and brown sugar, rolled up and baked.

My personal favourite dessert (no sarcasm here) is *sucre à la crème*, another offensively fattening recipe, but for which I have found no other origin than plain old French Canada. *Sucre à la crème* is basically white sugar, brown sugar, butter and (wait for it) heavy cream, all mixed together, cooked until dangerously hot, then cooled down in the fridge and cut into squares of absolute guilty pleasure. *Sucre à la crème* is also used as a spread, and extreme sugar lovers can stuff the mixture into pie pastry and make a *tarte au sucre*. Of course, this pie is not complete if not served with fresh cream and a signed contract for Weight Watchers. Sugar being relatively cheap, *sucre à la crème* often replaced the more expensive maple syrup, which even today remains a pretty pricy sugary liquid. As a side note, maple syrup is now on our table because of the Natives, who showed the first French Canadians how to extract the sap from maple trees. Let's face it, pinning a tree in the middle of winter for the juice running in it is not the first thing people would have thought about back then. Maple syrup has become the trademark product of Québec and has made a trip to a sugar shack the best outing one could ask for in the last months of winter. As a true French Canadian, I had my wedding reception at a sugar shack (and no, we were not wearing plaid shirts and dancing jigs), and for guests coming from elsewhere, it was a culinary experience they will remember forever.

So, French Canadians have invented some foods and adapted many recipes from their French ancestors to use whatever ingredients could be found in the New World. From fancy crème Chantilly to indescribable poutine, the French Canadian diet is sure to offer everyone a taste of the French influence in Canada (and perhaps a slight weight gain).

Canadians are experts in French food, indeed. But I think what we like more than food is probably drink, and the French brought over several fun things to drink. Of course, the French are best known for their wine, but beer was actually the first thing brewed in Canada, simply because the cold weather was perfect for keeping beer at a somewhat cool temperature, whereas wine had to be kept in a dry but warmer environment. Also, the weather here was really tricky for anyone who wished to grow grape vines to make good-quality wine, an almost impossible feat until at least the 1970s. Back in the 1600s, Recollet priests prepared beer in a caldron and kept it for themselves. This might have been a sin because I was taught that every Christian was supposed to share.

Back in France (and most of Europe), beer had been part of the diet for several centuries, at least since the Egyptians figured out how to make barley interesting. The people who ended up coming here, priests, farmers and children alike, had been drinking beer all their lives, starting with a healthy breakfast of dried bread and a pint of the devil's liquid. Water in those days was considered, if not dangerous, at least mysterious enough that people stayed away from it. Water was believed to carry germs, or at least this was the reason given to avoid bathing and to have a beer first thing in the morning. The effects of alcohol were considered medicinal, and being drunk was not as taboo as it eventually became. Alcohol was, more than water, the solution to every ailment, and was prescribed to every member of the family, children included. Beer was the equivalent of a glass of water today, and we see beer the way they used to see water, though it's a good thing we don't use beer for our baths.

Several home breweries opened in New France, one recorded as l'Abitation in Québec, which offered beer to locals. Unfortunately, it was destroyed by fire shortly after it opened. A decree in 1650 allowed small commercial breweries to operate, but we can thank Jean Talon, a French colonial administrator, for building the first real brewery a couple of decades later. Talon grew the hops necessary for beer production on his seigneurie and called his brewery La Brasserie du Roy. But French interest in spending money on the colony was not consistent, and after Talon returned to France, the brewery was dismantled. I guess beer was not always a Canadian priority.

Beer brewing dates back to ancient Roman times, but it was during medieval times that it really evolved, thanks to, yes, priests and monks. Charlemagne, the creator of schools, considered beer an essential part of life and took it upon himself to train people to brew good beer. This convinces me to forgive him for creating schools. Although Canadians are proud to be known for their love of beer, it is a shame that a majority of the beer we drink is produced by foreign multinationals. Even Sleemans, who once had the most sympathetic CEO ever, is now owned by the Japanese makers of Sapporo beer. At least, we can still boast that the French are the ones who brought it and drank it here first.

In 1992, a well-known Québec singer, Robert Charlebois, bought some shares in a brewery that had been declining and, with the help of two partners, renamed it Unibroue and moved its facilities to Chambly. There, they created a line of beers that are more of an experience than just a cold drink to accompany a hockey game. La Maudite, La Blanche de Chambly and La Don de dieu are all strong beers that are fermented and refermented to give them a special taste.

Although wine is the brew the French are known for, this beverage did not really have a substantial influence on the creation of Canada. However, we could say that we owe the political creation of Canada, Confederation, to inebriation. Indeed, it is a running gag among historians (yes, I know, we are quite boring) that the many conferences that resulted in the signing of the Constitution were accompanied by parties and even more drinking. Making the connection, people say that the Fathers of

Confederation were able to agree with each other because they were drunk most of the time during the negotiations. It could also be said that the country was conquered because of an another import, *eau de vie* (literally "water of life"; distilled alcohol). This strong liquor was an abomination for the Native population, who rapidly took up the habit of drinking it, although not as carefully as the Europeans had perhaps grown used to doing.

Another fine French creation that we still enjoy today is cognac, named for the town in which it is produced. Yet another type of liqueur brought to Canada by the French is triple sec, which we rarely drink on its own, but rather mix it with other alcohol or fruit juice. One of my favourite liqueurs is made out of both triple sec and cognac, and is called Grand Marnier. It has been served in France since the 1880s. Because of the free trade that went on soon after the founding of the colony and continued until well after Grand Marnier came along, French Canadians were able to obtain two of their favourite drinks—Jamaican rum and French brandy—relatively easily. These two beverages were readily available and cheaper to buy than the beer the colonists were producing themselves. All of these are still staples in Canadian bars and have contributed, in a twisted way, to helping Canadians connect with (and marry) each other since the country's beginning. Elaborate wine glasses dating back to the 17th century were found in Québec City, which demonstrates that Champlain was a *bon vivant* and made sure his people could enjoy themselves. There is a record of Champlain actually complaining about the cold weather because it froze the booze, and it had to be distributed by the pound rather than by the ounce.

Drinking was not a major problem in the French colony apart from the usual exceptional bouts of drunkenness and the numerous occasions for drinking. Habits changed, however, when their English counterparts took over and established themselves; the result wasn't pretty. Drinking alcohol was a habit as cheap as drinking water—Canadians used alcohol as a remedy for pretty much everything, even to stop a baby from crying. Not that the French were any better than the English, but with the strong Catholic hold on the personal lives of French Canadians, drunkenness was frowned upon and considered a sin. By 1851, there were 1990 taverns in Upper Canada, which was one for every 478 people. It seems that early Canadians preferred taverns to saloons, though there doesn't seem to have been a clear distinction between the two (some historians say that taverns used to offer rooms for sleeping upstairs—spotless and tidy rooms, I am sure). The French drinkers and the Catholic

Church were not great companions, however, and an anti-drinking crusade, led by Father Charles Chiniquy, went through French Canada. Within two years, Chiniquy was able to convince some 200,000 French Canadians to give up alcohol permanently. The movement eventually died down after the excommunication of Chiniquy, who was accused of improper behaviour towards members of the female sex. How ironic. I guess he couldn't blame booze for that.

Towards the end of the 19th century, Canadian drinking habits changed, and consuming alcohol became more of a recreational activity. It was no longer a central element of the diet and appeared less often in the middle of the dinner table. Canadians started drinking less for a good reason—alcohol was forbidden in the workplace, which meant that some 60 hours a week could now not be dedicated to drinking. The notable exceptions were soldiers, who were allowed to drink whenever they pleased; if they were going to sacrifice their lives for the nation, who could justify taking the booze away from them? Slowly, the concept of "moderation" came into being and has since remained. Today, Canadians still like their beer, but they are much more reasonable drinkers than their predecessors.

CHAPTER FIFTEEN

FRENCH CANADIANS AND SPORTS

The French influence is really everywhere, from theatre to food to drinking alcohol. There is yet another department in which French Canadians do pretty well—sports. Of course, being the first Europeans here, they were the first to play their own games on the continent. No early documentation exists, but we could probably safely assume that the French were the first ones to witness a game played by the Natives, with netted racquets used to pick up a ball and throw it. The game was a method of training the young and also a sort of religious ritual. But considering how clueless early explorers were when it came to understanding other cultures, the game side of it was probably all they could comprehend. Jesuit missionary Jean de Brébeuf wrote about the game in 1636 and called it lacrosse, only because the game involved a stick called a *crosse* in French. The (less than original) name stuck, and the sport is played today more than ever. In its Native origins, hundreds of players played at one time, and games were said to last for days. It was a (relatively) peaceful way to resolve conflicts between tribes, and it certainly kept a lot of people busy chasing a ball up and down a field. I assume there was more than one ball used in a game of 100 players, but maybe it was just the most challenging ball-chasing game ever. The first lacrosse association was started in Montréal by Dr. William George Beers (not an intentional link to the previous chapter). There are now lacrosse federations throughout the world, playing either field lacrosse or box lacrosse (indoors).

Some argue that hockey evolved from lacrosse, an adaptation of the Native game and the European tendency to take something, change it a bit and call it their own. However, there are many theories about how hockey was born, and lacrosse seems to be a far-fetched jump between the two sports. The Irish game of hurling is a more probable origin because it was closer to the game we know, using a curved stick, a ball and no throwing.

French Canadians cannot be credited for playing the first game of hockey. Rather, it was a group of students from McGill University who were the first to play in a recorded game in 1875. French Canadians started playing some 20 years later, when the sport was introduced by the priests who taught in schools. Hockey was at first a distinguished sport for wealthy English Canadians, but when their French counterparts started playing, the sport lost its "fancyness." Assuming that French Canadians were poorer and perhaps rougher around the edges, their game must have been less distinguished, indeed. The fact that players began to earn money took away any interest on the part of the English to continue playing. Once the sport became a paid job instead of an exclusive pastime, French Canadians became more numerous on the ice. Although they didn't play the sport first, the French are responsible for the creation of a hockey dynasty that is either loved or hated by every hockey fan in Canada, the United States and perhaps in every hockey-playing country in the world.

For the first five years of the team's existence, only Francophone players were recruited to play for the Montréal Canadiens. The team was created specifically to employ French Canadians and to create a rivalry between the English and the French. There was already an English-speaking team in the city, and wealthy industrialist J. Ambrose O'Brien wanted to spice things up a bit, so in 1909, the Montréal Canadiens were created. There was another French team at the time, the Nationals, though no one knows why that team was not recruited to play against Montréal's English team. The first English-speaking member of the Canadiens, James "Rocket" Power, was hired despite an outcry from French Montréalers. Other teams who wanted Francophone players to play for them had to ask permission from the Montréal Canadiens management.

The team is nicknamed the Habs (for *habitants*), but is also know as *Le Bleu-Blanc-Rouge*, *Les Glorieux* and *La sainte flanelle*, a mix of religion (which was always very important) and comfort (*flanelle* is what pyjamas are made of). The Montréal Canadiens celebrate their centenary in 2009, and the team has grown from a small "garage" team to a real institution. French Canadians have always been big fans of hockey, a trait that unifies them throughout Canada.

French Canada has produced many hockey heroes, and since hockey is our national sport, I will dwell on some of them for a bit. (The fact that I have spent three years studying a Canadiens player, or have presented the history of hockey in countless conferences, or married a descendant of Toe Blake has nothing to do with it, I swear.) The first star of the Montréal

Canadiens was undoubtedly Newsy Lalonde, a player from Cornwall, Ontario. Although he did not speak a word of French, he is usually considered the first French player, because of his name. Lalonde was also a star lacrosse player, and he is credited for having scored the first goal in the NHL (because he played in the first game after the league's creation). Lalonde wasn't a "true" Canadien in the sense that French Canadians mean it. He changed teams several times, playing for the team that offered him the most money. A "real" Canadien was a player who spent his whole career on the team and had "C-H" tattooed on his heart, figuratively speaking, of course. The first Francophone legend to play with the team was Aurèle Joliat, who played 16 seasons with the Habs, but retired relatively early in 1938 after the death of his teammate, Howie Morenz, broke his heart.

Perhaps the biggest star of the Montréal Canadiens, and a symbol for French Canadians throughout the province and perhaps the country, was Maurice "Rocket" Richard. Richard started playing for the Montréal Canadiens during World War II, at a time when the team was really not doing well. He broke every scoring record there was and became the first player ever to score 50 goals in 50 games. He came to be seen as a true French Canadian hero after the riots of 1955—he was the lone Frenchman in a sea of corporate Englishmen. He spent his life telling people he was only a hockey player, but he received honours that went beyond his hockey fame. He received the Order of Canada and of Québec, and was named to the Queen's Privy Council. When he died, the Rocket was allowed state funeral, a privilege usually reserved for political figures. Other players, for example Mario Lemieux and Guy Lafleur, have since broken his records, but some of these players were also French Canadians, thus "keeping it in the family." Two other players, Jean Béliveau and Émile "Butch" Bouchard, have followed in Rocket Richard's footsteps, being honoured by the provincial government for their work both on and off the ice. They have both received the Order of Québec, Bouchard having received it recently. All this to say that although the French were not the first to play the game of hockey, they were certainly the first to break records and make hockey the hotbed of superstars it is now. The Montréal Canadiens now have only a small number of French Canadians on the team, but whenever they play against the Toronto Maple Leafs, the games always take on an "English vs. French" rivalry. My husband went to one of these games in Montréal, and after the Canadiens suffered a humiliating loss to the Leafs, some disappointed fans screamed at the red-white-and-blue crowd that they were a bunch of separatists.

Never mind that the proportion of Anglophone and Francophone fans of the Habs must be about the same, the team is still considered a symbol of the French Canadian population.

Besides having the coolest hockey hero and the most legendary team, the French have scored some other firsts. The first telecast of a hockey game was in French, in Montréal, in 1952, and the first covered ice rink in the world was built in Québec City in 1842. French Canadians are as crazy about hockey as any other Canadian, and if you asked real hockey fans what the most important influence of the French on hockey was, you would get a pretty standard answer—goaltenders. Apparently, French Canada has grown powerful enough to genetically modify its population in order to make amazing goaltenders out of ordinary people. Joking aside, some of the best goaltenders in the NHL today and throughout history have been French Canadians: Patrick Roy, Martin Brodeur and Jacques Plante, to name just a few.

The French influence in sports goes beyond Canada's national sport, of course. One of the fields in which French Canadians have made their mark is linked directly to their origins as *coureurs des bois* and then as lumberjacks. Indeed, French Canada has produced some of the best-known strongmen, wrestlers and boxers. The most notable strongman was

perhaps Louis Cyr, a world-renowned, mous-
tachioed Québec native. The fact that he was
among the first to make a living out of his odd
talent has made him a legend. But because he
performed his feats in the late 1800s, at a time
when there were no cameras to provide photo-
graphic evidence of his feats, some of his
records have been exaggerated. Cyr did impress
the world with his sheer strength, resisting the
pull of four horses on one occasion and lifting
a platform with 18 men on it on another. When
he retired as a strongman, he became a police
officer. I can guess that whomever he arrested
did not argue and followed him to the police
station without a word. Louis Cyr was the first,
but many other French Canadians have influenced Canada's reputation as a producer of
strongmen.

France can historically be credited as being
the first place where people wrestled. Ever.
Indeed, cave drawings dating back some
15,000 years were found in a French cave, and
apparently what is depicted in these drawings,
among other things, is two men wrestling. So
in a strangely historic way, the French influence in wrestling is important. As good descendants, French Canadians have been quite
present on the wrestling scene: Yvon Robert,
the Rougeau brothers and Maurice "Mad Dog"
Vachon are only a few of the men who have
made careers out of hurting other people in

a weird but entertaining way. Vachon was probably the first one to start the "trash talk" strategy that is now part of pro wrestling. He would give interviews before a fight and talk about how bad his opponents were and how good he was. This was great publicity and a way to guarantee that tempers would be running high on fight night. Vachon was a marketer before people like Vince MacMahon, president of the WWE (World Wrestling Entertainment, Inc.). The Rougeau brothers were also known for having a similar unsportsmanlike attitude, becoming a hated duo on purpose. The brothers did things outside the ring to make sure fans disliked them, and they did pretty well because they were often booed when they finally showed up to fight. American fans didn't like the fact that the Rougeaus pretended to be Americans and would threaten to go live in Tennessee. French Canadians in Tennessee? What an awful crime. Canadians sure know how to push Americans' buttons.

From hockey, a winter sport, to wrestling, an arguably summery confrontation, now to a sports gathering for both seasons—the Olympics. The French were certainly not the first to think about holding a worldwide contest for national showboating, but it is to a Frenchman that we owe our modern Olympic games. Pierre de Coubertin, a French aristocrat, believed that sharing national talents in a friendly competition was the true essence of free trade:

> Let us export our oarsmen, our runners, our fencers into other lands. That is the true Free Trade of the future; and the day it is introduced into Europe the cause of Peace will have received a new and strong ally. It inspires me to touch upon another step I now propose [...] the splendid and beneficent task of reviving the Olympic Games.

So de Coubertin ended up convincing the right people to revive the legendary Olympics, and the first Games took place in April 1896, appropriately in Athens, Greece. His Canadian cousins have made him proud by participating, and winning, numerous Olympic medals. A list of the French Canadians who have won medals for Canada would be too long to include here, but let's look at some of the most notable performances. In the end, this book is about how the French have influenced the nation as a whole, and what better way to show patriotism than by winning a medal in the name of Canada.

Étienne Desmarteau was probably the first Canadian ever to win an Olympic gold medal, a feat he accomplished in the 1904 Summer Olympics held in St. Louis, Missouri. It has been argued that there was a Canadian gold medallist in the Olympics in 1900, but because he competed for the United States, I think we can safely say that Desmarteau was really the first one. True to the tradition of strong lumber-jacks, Desmarteau won a strength contest, throwing a 56-pound (25.4-kilogram) weight a record 34 feet (10.3 metres). Why a 56-pound weight and not one with a round number is beyond me. Apparently, the event was taken out of the Olympics shortly after Desmarteau won the medal. We don't know how he threw the weight, but we do know that there were no restrictions as to the throwing method. Today, very delicate (insert sly, sarcastic smile here) athletes spin around a few times and use momentum to throw the weight. In Desmart-eau's time, he could do the same, or throw it like a rookie bowler (between the legs) or even run for a while and then throw it. Either way, he broke a record and has gone down in history. He almost didn't go to the Olympics because his employer, the Montréal police force, did not want to pay him during his leave of absence. Although he did get fired for leaving, his employer rehired him right away when he returned with a gold medal. The Montréal police department realized belatedly how important the Olympics were.

Jump forward to 2002, when a French Cana-dian, paired up with his partner from Ontario, was responsible for a serious inquiry into Olympic judging. After a perfect performance in the pairs figure skating event in Salt Lake City, David Pelletier and wife and partner Jamie Salé graciously received a silver medal, although the fans were a little less than gracious, booing the medal ceremony because they thought the pair should have won the gold. This could have been just another story of disappointed Canadians, but a huge scandal erupted in the Olympic world. A French judge (no link to French Canadians here) had been "encouraged" by another judge to vote for the Russians instead of Pelletier and Salé, and in exchange, that same judge promised to vote for the French team in another competition. Because of the controversy, the Canadian pair was given a gold medal as well, the first time that two gold medals were awarded for the same event. The judging in figure skating has since been changed to make it less subjective, meaning that Pelletier and Salé were instrumental in changing the face of international figure skating.

Another notable French Olympian is Chantal Petitclerc, a wheelchair athlete who has won more than a dozen Paralympic medals and one Olympic medal. She has since become something of a Canadian celebrity, getting calls to host shows, awards ceremonies and conferences. For the longest time, she was also the announcer of lotto numbers on TV. Canada has a knack for finding all kinds of jobs for its Olympians.

CHAPTER SIXTEEN

FRENCH CANADIANS MEAN BUSINESS

The French influence in Canada can be found not only in culture and sports, but also in business. Because French is not the language of business, even in Canada, it must be something of a surprise to learn that several French Canadians have had a great influence on Canadian economics, in different ways. French Canadians were not traditionally very present in the business world—the Conquest of 1760 had isolated them; the Great Depression had not given them a chance. In the rare instances when French Canadians did well, they were confined to the province of Québec, which didn't help them to gain national recognition.

A good example of this was Gabriel-Alphonse Desjardins, who founded the Caisses populaires Desjardins in 1900, a French Canadian financial institution with offices throughout central and eastern Canada. Desjardins realized that it wasn't possible for "ordinary" citizens to borrow money from existing financial institutions because these banks only lent large sums to wealthy people. A particular legal case had resonated with him—a man had been charged some $1500 of interest on a $150 loan by a usurer. Desjardins sought to change the awful practice of usury, which was, at that time, the only option for ordinary people who sometimes ended up a bit short of cash once in a while. What the *caisse*, or credit union, offered was simple—by buying a five-dollar share, every member was entitled to take loans from the larger sum that was amassed this way. It was sort of a communal account into which people put their small savings, allowing them access to larger sums if they needed them. For Desjardins, the concept of the *caisse* was like a parish—a tight-knit community of savvy French Canadian savers:

> The *caisse populaire* is truly an organization of the parish. It was born, nourished and developed in the midst of the parochial family, and that is where it thrives. The parish is its natural birthplace, the

focus of its activities...Economically speaking, it is, in a word, the extension of the parish.

The parish had religious and geographical limits, so it is no surprise that the Church supported the idea, notwithstanding the fact that Desjardins was a committed Catholic. The Church helped Desjardins to establish the first *caisse* in Lévis, Québec, and priest Phillipe Grondin dedicated himself to "selling" the concept elsewhere in the province. Just to show how involved the Church was, the priest wrote a pamphlet explaining how the *caisse* worked. The pamphlet, entitled *Le catechisme de la caisse populaire* (The Catechism of the Credit Union), was reminiscent of the religious teachings that French Catholics had to learn in school. It took many years before the company was able to extend its operations outside Québec, but today there are Desjardins establishments throughout Québec as well as in Ontario, Manitoba, New Brunswick and even the United States with close to five million shareholders. Desjardins still prides itself on offering personalized service *en français* to its customers, even in the U.S. The reason that Desjardins started to do business across the border was to serve the growing population of French Canadians who moved to Florida. When French Canadians travel, we not only take our shorts with the

Canadian flag printed on them but also our financial institutions.

Most of the businessmen who achieved national recognition did so after World War II. It seems that French Canadians had finally gotten a taste of what capitalism was and wanted a piece of the action. One of the first to jump on the bandwagon was an inventor from Québec. Fifty years ago, Joseph-Armand Bombardier invented a snow-car in a garage because he wanted people to be able to move around even during winter—a vehicle created in response to our Canadian climate, which had until then ruled how and when people travelled. After inventing the Ski-Doo, the company achieved worldwide success, and production increased rapidly. Because of the petroleum crisis of the 1970s, Bombardier had to reduce its production because people were less inclined to spend money on gas for a recreational vehicle (sounds familiar in today's economy). This forced the company to start looking elsewhere to make money. Bombardier began to make equipment for the Montréal metro and produced such high-quality cars that New York subway executives asked that their cars be made by Bombardier as well. Since then, the company has become known not only for Ski-Doos and metro cars, but also Sea-Doos, trains and airplanes. From a small garage in Valcourt, Québec, Bombardier became a leader in transportion equipment and has offices throughout the world.

Pierre Péladeau is another notable businessman, the French Canadian equivalent of Conrad Black minus the legal problems. Péladeau was interested in the media and became the owner of a small newspaper that was doing poorly. After his purchase, Péladeau founded a company called Québecor in 1950 and started producing two newspapers, one for Montréal and one for Québec City. He profited from a newspaper strike by creating his own paper—a great marketing move, but one that must have angered the striking journalists. The two newspapers did pretty well and are still among the most widely read in Québec. Péladeau understood very quickly that most of a newspaper's profit is usually spent outsourcing part of the production process, so he bought a pulp-and-paper company to produce the paper on which his news was printed—a bold move in the 1980s. Québecor eventually stepped into televised media and purchased a TV network serving Québec. In 1999, the company also purchased Sun media, which produces the *Calgary, Edmonton, Ottawa, Toronto* and *Vancouver Sun* newspapers, among many others. This single purchase made Québecor the largest publishing company in Canada (Québecor Inc.), and it is also the second largest printing company in the world (Québecor World). Although it is a huge operation, Québecor is still run by the family, Péladeau's son having taken over after his father's death in 1997.

Paul Desmarais is from Sudbury, Ontario, and is today the fifth wealthiest Canadian. He began his career by taking over his parents' company, the Sudbury Bus Line, in 1951. After several purchases and some share-exchange programs, Desmarais ended up owner of Power Corporation, which holds companies in Canada, the United States, Europe and Asia. It owns, among others, the Great West and London Life Insurance companies, Mackenzie Financial Services and Investors Group. More interesting than Desmarais' financial success are the people he befriends. Desmarais counts among his best friends Paul Martin, Jean Chrétien, Brian Mulroney and the late Pierre Trudeau. Interestingly, these are all people who were employed by Power Corp before they began their political careers. Paul Martin became tremendously wealthy after partnering with Desmarais; Jean Chretien's name has figured on the board of directors of Power Corp and his daughter married one of Desmarais' sons; Trudeau was on an advisory board for the corporation; and Mulroney has provided legal services to Desmarais. So whomever Desmarais befriends seems to have a pretty good chance of becoming prime minister. Although this shows how business inclined our PMs are, it also demonstrates how powerful this French Canadian from Subdury has become.

The Nickel Capital was also the home of another influential financier, Robert Campeau, who deals in real estate. He started his career by building housing for civil servants in Ottawa in the 1950s, though the mayor of the city always thought his construction looked absolutely awful. Considering how wealthy Campeau was at one point, perhaps ugly buildings are the way to go. He has been a tad less successful than Desmarais, if only because his company at one point owned Bloomingdale's but could not meet its financial obligations and had to declare bankruptcy. Lucky for Campeau, he had "gifted" all of his assets to his wife, so when creditors came knocking on his door, they had to turn around empty-handed. For some, Campeau has had a negative influence on the economics of Canada, as evidenced by the title of a book by John Rothchild, *Going for Broke: How Robert Campeau Bankrupted the Retail Industry, Jolted the Junk Bond Market and Brought the Booming '80s to a Crashing Halt.* Even in Berlin, Germany, where he "retired" after the Bloomingdale fiasco, the tabloids referred to him as Mr. Bankrupt. But in the end, Campeau was never bankrupt himself and remains an important figure in the

Canadian building industry, as he still works in Toronto.

There are many other influential French Canadians such as Jean Coutu, the man who founded the Pharmacies Jean Coutu franchise. Jean Coutu has become a household name in Québec, but the company operates under different names in New Brunswick, Ontario and the United States.

Another French Canadian success is the communications firm Cossette, originally a graphics studio located in Québec City. It was revamped as a communications and marketing firm and was able to get contracts with important Canadian companies such as Bell Canada, General Motors Canada and McDonald's Restaurants Canada. The small firm eventually grew into a national company with offices in Toronto and Vancouver. Cossette Communications, a subsidiary of the group, operates in New York, and the group has recently purchased a marketing firm based in Los Angeles. So besides inventing the quintessential comfort food (poutine) and creating a hockey dynasty, French Canadians have also changed the economic landscape of the nation. Plus, these financial tycoons are also entertaining, which is not common occurrence in the financial world.

CHAPTER SEVENTEEN

FRENCH CANADIAN POLITICS

The French *joie de vivre* is not a myth, and the proof is that French Canadians make whatever they do cool and entertaining, business included. French Canada is as proliferate with politicians as it is with goaltenders and tycoons. Canadian prime ministers Wilfrid Laurier, Louis St. Laurent, Pierre Trudeau and Jean Chrétien were and are French Canadians, while Brian Mulroney comes from Québec and John Abbott is buried here. We breed them, and we bury them.

Wilfrid Laurier, the first French Canadian prime minister, worked hard not only to expand the number of territories in the Confederation, but also to resolve the problems between

English and French Canadians. His hard work earned him a place on our five-dollar bill, and considering the current economic crisis, it is quite an honour to have your face on bills that may become scarce in the years to come. Laurier did well in school, earned a law degree and got married, becoming a dedicated statesman. Even his extramarital affair with his partner's wife was deemed "platonic," and people were not at all incensed by it. Or perhaps the notorious unfaithfulness of American politicians was an accepted fact here in Canada. Laurier had dreamed of becoming a politician and remained devoted to politics until his death in 1919. When his party suffered a staggering loss after World War I, Laurier tried to rebuild the Liberals but died before he could achieve his goal. There is a funny anecdote about Laurier and a paperboy. Getting off a train, Laurier rushed to purchase a newspaper to see what was going on. He started to chat with the paperboy who, after a while, told Laurier he had wasted enough time on him and had to go sell more newspapers. To add to this, the newspaper boy was John Diefenbaker, who would become prime minister himself some 40 years later. This anecdote adds to Laurier's image as a man who was humble despite his status.

Louis St. Laurent was the 12th Canadian prime minister and was the opposite of Laurier. He was Minister of Justice in Québec, and when World War II began, William Lyon Mac-kenzie King asked him to be part of his war-time cabinet. St. Laurent accepted, with the condition that as soon as the war was over, he could go back to doing what he was doing. He became prime minister following the retire-ment of Mackenzie King. Laurier was influen-tial in helping detach Canada from Britain, at least politically and legally. He was a conscien-tious politician, and after the war ended, he used tax surpluses to pay the national debt in full. He was the only prime minister that can boast of having repaid our debt completely. He is affectionately known as "Uncle Louis," a nickname given to him during his political campaigning. Apparently, his party was afraid that St. Laurent was too old to appeal to peo-ple. By making him sympathetic, they thought he would resonate more with the public, hence the friendly name Uncle Louis. This idea came from observing him getting off a train and heading towards a group of young kids instead of going to see a group of journalists and politi-cians who were waiting for him. Then again, who could blame him for choosing children over politicians.

Pierre Elliott Trudeau should have a chapter to himself because he was so entertaining. Who else in Canadian political history has had "mania" attached to his last name? Trudeau made politics sexy, but he also made French

Canada something other than a closed community afraid to open up. Trudeau had a hand in the Quiet Revolution, editing a journal, *Cité Libre*, that condemned Duplessis' overbearing rule. When working as Minister of Justice, he passed a bill that decriminalized homosexuality, abortion, contraception and lotteries, and he softened divorce laws. All in all, much of what the world knows of Canada is owed directly to Trudeau. He was also a joker, as we have seen when he danced behind the Queen, sparking wild interpretations that he meant to ridicule the British government. We owe bilingualism to Trudeau and also the strong repression of the October Crisis, which made it only an October crisis rather than a 1970 one.

The fourth and (to date) last Francophone prime minister was Jean Chrétien. While we have heard so many negative things about the man, underlining occasions when he looked ridiculous, he was a tremendous influence on Canada, if only by making inconsequential mistakes. A hat worn backwards, the attempted strangling of a man in front of cameras, his strong and unrepentant French accent—Chrétien showed us how relaxed he was about the whole thing and, perhaps, what a normal guy he was. Think about it—if you were followed constantly, you would eventually be caught saying or doing something stupid. His missteps made Chrétien appear sympathetic rather than simple, and his work as a politician cannot be disregarded. He was mocked because of his speech impediment and facial disfigurement; most people do not realize that these were caused by a stroke when he was young and were an actual handicap. The failed referendum was hailed by many as a victory for Chrétien, while others have interpreted this as an almost loss. He was criticized mostly for inaction, and scandals marred an otherwise positive legacy. Nevertheless, Chrétien put the small city of Shawinigan on the map, and he also represented a good portion of the Francophone community—those who were rural and not wealthy. He was a different kind of prime minister, and probably closer to the French Canadian people than any other.

While the above-mentioned French Canadians have shaped Canadian politics as a whole, the first "politicians" in the country were all Frenchmen—the governors and governors general of New France. And since, at that time, ruling over people was less structured and definitely less scrutinized, it made for quite interesting leaders.

The first governor of New France after Champlain was Charles Huault de Montmagny. Governor of the colony from 1636 to 1648, Montmagny was a French aristocrat, but most importantly, he was a member of the Knights of Malta. Why was that important? The

Knights were, in effect, Christian pirates. The order was first created as part of the Crusade movement in 1065, but lost its purpose after the Conquest of Jerusalem. So in 1530, their grandmaster had the genius idea of selling their services to the Catholic Church to help monitor the surrounding seas for heathen Ottoman Turks. This essentially made them pirates because they took prisoners and stole the goods they found on ships, but since they were Christian, it was all considered just. And because the Knights were unwavering in their support of the Church, when it was time to send people overseas to provide order in a new colony, they were the first ones on the list. The first ruler of New France, then, was a Knight whose order had participated in the Crusades.

The next governor worth talking about was perhaps the most controversial (and also the one with the longest name): Louis de Buade de Frontenac et de Palluau, who would have had to have the widest hockey jersey ever to fit all of his name. He was governor general of New France from 1672 to 1682 and then again from 1689 to 1698. Frontenac was a big spender, and by the time the French king appointed him governor, he was in serious debt. He had secretly married a soon-to-be wealthy heiress, but when her father found out, he disinherited her, so both Frontenac and his wife were, well, broke. He took on an appointment in Crete and then the one in New France mostly to evade his creditors. Shortly after arriving in the colony, he established a fur-trading post in his own name without asking anyone. If anyone complained, he had them arrested, and the rest of the population was put on *corvée* and forced to build the fort for the trading post. *Corvée*, or "chore" in English, means doing a task for someone because they ask you to (a concept that seems too complicated to understand for children aged 10 to 18). Since the 16th century, however, *corvée* had been become forced labour. Rulers would ask their subjects to build a road or tend a garden or anything else—to be done in their spare time and, of course, for free. By Frontenac's time, *corvée* was becoming a point of contention between the French king and his subjects, as the amount of work asked of people was growing. Add this to the constant warring (and need for soldiers), and the French people must have been tired of working for free. In any case, Frontenac decided to use the concept of *corvée* in New France in order to get things going, and he was successful in this. Indeed, the seigneurial system, which remained the basis of Québec's society for centuries, continued to use the *corvée* as a way to develop the *seigneurie* by building mills and churches, among other things.

Frontenac constantly fought with the clergy and the colony's intendant. The clergy had as much power as the governor general, and it wasn't clear where each one's powers ended. The disagreements between Frontenac and members of the clergy were mostly about who was allowed to do what. The intendant position had been "invented" in New France in 1665, and it basically consisted of appointing someone to keep the governor in check and report on his actions to the king of France. The intendant was a kind of spy/tattletale, and it was inevitable that someone like Frontenac would find issues to fight about. He constantly bickered with the clergy, and the intendant got him recalled to France, but the influence of his wife eventually allowed him to return to New France for another term as governor general. In the end, he succeeded in reducing the number of Iroquois attacks on the colony, and he expanded the fur trade to reach western Canada. And who can really blame him for living extravagantly, when even today we seem to catch political figures spending our money heedlessly.

Between Frontenac's two terms, Jacques-René Brisay de Denonville ruled the colony from 1685 to 1689. What we remember Denonville for is his lack of fear. He reconquered several forts that had belonged to New France but were taken by the British. He also tricked an entire Iroquois council and ended up sending all of them to France for enslavement. The result was a violent response from the Iroquois. They burned down the village of Lachine, a couple of miles west of Montréal. As a result, Denonville was recalled to France, but his campaigns to return territory to New France rule warranted him a good job—tutor to the King's children. This means he tutored Louis XV, the king originally nicknamed "the Beloved." Louis XV is remembered as one of the worst kings of France, mostly because of his lack of morals (he had the most famous mistress in history, Madame de Pompadour) and his failure to rule the country effectively. I wonder what Denonville taught him.

Marquis Philippe Rigaud de Vaudreuil was another notable governor general who ruled the colony from 1703 to 1725, and he was much less controversial than Frontenac. He succeeded in upholding the peace with the Iroquois and worked towards an immigration program to populate the country. His son Pierre would be the last governor of New France and was a bit more entertaining than his father. He had previously been governor of Louisiana, though when he took the position, he had no idea what it entailed. His small salary could not sustain his extravagant lifestyle, so he purchased a plantation and some 30 slaves to work for him. When he left, he sold the plantation for a huge profit, but he had also tripled the revenues of the colony. As governor general of New France, Vaudreuil had the unfortunate legacy of being the one who surrendered the territory to the British. And France was looking for a scapegoat, so Vaudreuil was put on trial in France. His name was eventually cleared, but during the trial, both a brother and his wife died and he was inconsolable.

CHAPTER EIGHTEEN

FRENCH CANADA, FRANCE AND THE REST OF THE WORLD...OR UNIVERSE

Canada was at first a French colony, under the rule of the government of France. Until the Conquest of 1760, France was the ruler, the faraway government that dictated how life was to be conducted in New France. It was after the Conquest that the relationship between the two countries began to change, and not in the same way through-out the nation. New France, which eventually became Québec, kept a close link to its over-seas cousins, as they seemed to be its only companions amid a sea of British subjects. There was also some resentment, though, as France had agreed to give up the colony and leave it to its own fate. It was only in 1854 that France showed renewed interest in its abandoned colony. A ship named *La Capricieuse* landed in Québec City with the purpose of rekindling the link between the two nations and reestablishing commercial relations with Canada.

The rest of Canada was peopled primarily with people of British descent, quickly making Canada a predominantly English-speaking country. At the same time that Canada tried to break out from under British rule to assert itself as a country, Québec did the same, which was illustrated by the province sending its own representative to France to defend its rights. Still under British rule, Canada was involved in World War I, and many Canadian soldiers ended up fighting in France, saving the territory of their ancestors. However, the Canadian army was not set up to accommodate French soldiers—officers and administrators spoke only English, training was done in English, and documents were exclusively in English. To add to this, being involved in a war under the British, fighting for their conqueror, wasn't very enticing for French Canadians. In addition, it seemed that Francophones were less linked to France since the country had become more secular. While it was slowly losing its power, the Church was still a crucial part of French Canadians' lives, even in the early 20th century.

More than 15,000 French Canadians volunteered in World War I, and many of them were instrumental in the costly but decisive victory at Vimy Ridge. It became more difficult to find volunteers after a while, so the Canadian government decided to proceed with conscription, which didn't go over as well in Québec as it did in the rest of Canada. The debate prior to the adoption of conscription was tremendously bitter and was unfortunately clearly divided between the English and the French, a major setback for a relatively new country trying to remain unified. Conscription began in 1918, but of the 400,000 possible conscripts, 94 percent got out of it with some kind of exemption, and 98 percent did so in Québec. Close to 30,000 Canadians simply went into hiding or escaped to the United States, 18,000 of them from Québec. All in all, conscription brought in some 20,000 Canadian soldiers, but certainly put a dent in the idea of Canadian unity.

The same almost happened in World War II, sparked by the same problematic issues. In that worldwide conflict, Canada went to war on its own, and the French-speaking units did very well. The Fusilliers du Mont-Royal, the Royal 22e regiment, the Régiment de la Chaudière and others were instrumental in several key victories. The most important of these were probably D-Day and Operation

Overlord, or as it is called in French, the *Débarquement de Normandie*. In a way, French Canadian involvement in these military victories seemed to give something back to the region that had provided the first settlers to Canada. The landing at Juno Beach was the responsibility of Canadians, and they were the only ones to achieve their landing objectives. Canada had, of course, maintained a relationship with France during the war, but severed ties once France was taken over by Germany. However, once the Vichy government, a French government that collaborated with the Germans, was installed, Canada quickly recognized it as official and pursued diplomatic relations.

Charles de Gaulle was the leader of the "rebellious" Free French at the time, and when he visited Canada shortly after the war, crowds would chant "*Vive le Canada et vive la France!*" ("Long live Canada and long live France!"), illustrating how the relationship between the two countries had been rekindled. The next milestone in Canada-France relations happened in 1967, again with President de Gaulle. In the biggest misunderstanding ever, de Gaulle said to a huge crowd of Québec citizens who had voiced their discontent with the political situation at that time: "*Vive le Québec libre!*" ("Long live free Québec!"), which gave great impetus to the separatist movement, but dramatically cooled relations between the two countries, at least until de Gaulle resigned from his position. The fact that "*Québec libre*" became the slogan of the FLQ, the Front de Libération du Québec and the organization responsible for the October Crisis, probably did not help de Gaulle's cause in Canada. The closeness of de Gaulle and French Canada during the 1960s was responsible for the raucous relationship between Canada and France, mostly because of France's support for the separatist movement and its encouragement that the French from all the other provinces do the same. This seemed to be, for the English-speaking majority of the country, a) inappropriate interference in Canada's internal affairs, and b) an invitation to the French to work harder at breaking up the country.

With de Gaulle gone, relations with France returned to the distant politeness that currently exists. A small shadow remains on the otherwise positive link between France and Canada—the maritime boundary dispute involving the islands of St. Pierre and Miquelon. Because of interest in deep-sea drilling, this unresolved issue could eventually lead to a dispute. Nevertheless, Canada and France remain linked by their culture, and also by an ongoing stream of French immigrants to Canada. In the last five years, close to 20,000 French citizens have chosen Canada as their new home, proof that the New World is still drawing Europeans as a land of opportunity. Of course, the majority of them chose to establish themselves in Québec because of the language.

Canada and France are also linked by means of their participation in *La Francophonie*, an international consortium of French-speaking countries. Membership in the group is not determined by how much French is spoken, but rather how much French culture is present in the countries, which explains the membership of Romania, Moldavia and Egypt. Canada has representatives from Québec and New Brunswick who speak for their provinces, as well as an observer from Ontario, although that province has not yet signed up. Canada collaborates internationally in the promotion and development of French culture worldwide. Québec City, which celebrated its 400th anniversary in 2008, also hosted the twelfth summit of *La Francophonie*, illustrating how important Québec is in this international organization.

I mentioned in the title of this chapter that I would discuss French Canada and its relationship not only to the rest of the world, but also the universe. The reason for this is that there are two individuals that have made their mark in space. Marc Garneau was the first Canadian in space, and Julie Payette followed him a few years later. Garneau was a naval engineer who applied for the Canadian space program and was chosen from among 4000 applications. He went on three missions and became a well-known personality in Canada. After he left the space program, he used his popularity to enter politics. Garneau won a seat as the Liberal candidate for the Westmount riding in Montréal and now hovers over piles of paper instead of planets. Nevertheless, the journeys of two French Canadians into space takes French influence well beyond Canadian borders.

CONCLUSION

French culture in Canada has certainly not diminished despite being conquered by the British and being surrounded by English Canadians. Rather, it is the other cultures that have risen alongside the French, confirming Canada's national status as a mosaic, not a melting pot. It's not that there are fewer French people, it's more the fact that other communities have begun asserting themselves in a similar way, and thus have made the plight for cultural preservation more universal. The fact that the French legacy is kept alive indirectly strengthens the case for other cultures to be kept as vibrant and present, which is undoubtedly what encouraged communities to push for the recognition of their rights. Just before the 1995 referendum, Jean Chrétien made a speech that emphasized Canada's multiculturalism and the mutual respect among Canadians:

> What we have built together in Canada is something very great and very noble. A country whose values of tolerance, understanding, generosity have made us what we are: a society where our number one priority is the respect and dignity of all our citizens.

The French influence on Canada? It is the first piece in the Canadian mosaic. And the situation of the French in Canada seems comfortable despite a drop in proportion (28 to 23 percent of the population of Canada is Francophone), the French population is increasing, rising from 4.1 million to 6.8 million in 50 years. In 2001, 31 percent of Canadians could conduct a conversation in French, while 23 percent claimed French as their mother tongue. Not bad for a people conquered more than 300 years ago.

The development of the French population was very different depending on the geographical location of the community. But whether you are an Acadian or a Franco-Manitoban, I think it's safe to say that the same values motivate everyone's existence. Being French in

Canada was not always simple, and even today there are fights that need to be fought to secure French Canadians' rights somewhere. Resilience is, then, a common characteristic of the French in Canada—the will to fight to keep a culture that permeated the creation of the country. There is also toughness, whether physical or mental. Physical when we think of the lumberjacks and their pure force, but also the first settlers, battling the Canadian winter without adequate clothing, food or preparation. Mental because of the work that was needed to continue the legacy of these French settlers— political, artistic and communal fortitude was necessary. Finally, there is the idea of family, of community. French Canadians are very different from each other, yet they feel a certain degree of familiarity. Even if they are scattered throughout the country, they have worked, and still work, towards the common goal of keeping their traditions and culture alive. So, resilience, toughness and community. These are values that seem to me to be quintessentially Canadian, but I guess that should be no surprise. French Canadians are true Canadians, and they have contributed to the building of this nation in collaboration many other ethnic groups.

The French influence in Canada is everywhere, which made the writing of this book arduous, if only because I had to choose what to discuss and what to leave out. Because the French were the first Europeans in the country, their influence harkens back to the mid-17th century and that forces us to review our Canadian history. Society likes "firsts," and for this, French Canadians can boast of being the first to have done many things here in Canada, from agriculture to brewing beer to fighting one another with swords. This was also a problem for me, albeit a fun one—if the French were the first to do so many things, which ones to choose and, more importantly, how to research these firsts? Because they occurred so early in Canadian history, they have not been recorded in much detail. That is why I had to choose a) what I thought were important firsts in the making of Canada, and b) the ones that I could tell you a bit about! The fact that French communities are scattered throughout the country also requires us to study the whole nation's history.

I realized that my knowledge of Canadian history was Québec biased. It was what I had learned throughout my childhood and throughout my university studies. And I assume that it is the same for everyone in Canada, learning the general history of the country but concentrating on their province's own history. While the idea seems fair, I think we are missing out on very interesting histories when we only look at ourselves, and this was a sad realization for someone such as me who is studying history.

Trying to cover a nation's history was indeed a big task, but what we can take from all of this is that French influence is to be found everywhere, and it is kept alive through the continuing existence of French communities.

The future of the French in Canada is protected by laws and regulations and through the motivation of the people to keep the traditions alive. There is a certain pride in being historically old and also being able to say that we were the first to do this or that. It also means that we are all immigrants to this land. The Natives are actually the original inhabitants of Canada, and the French are as much a new people as any other immigrant group. It is the mixture of all the nationalities that makes Canada a mosaic—each culture is allowed to keep its language, its religion and its way of life. This is the primary reason that French Canadians are still thriving despite the Conquest; Canada has a long-standing tradition of letting its people be. Maybe the fact that we are all so different, coming from other nations or growing up in different communities, is what unites us—we represent how Canada is open to the world.

Notes on Sources

Arnopoulos, Sheila McLeod. *Voices from French Ontario.* Montréal: McGill-Queen's University Press, 1982.

Balian, Ohannes Sarkis. *The Caisse Populaire: A French-Canadian Economic Institution in Manitoba.* Winnipeg: University of Manitoba, 1975.

Benoit, Pierre. *Maisonneuve.* n.p., 1960.

Collet, Paulette. *40 ans de théâtre français à Toronto.* Mississauga: AnthropoMare, 2006.

Durieux, Marcel. *Ordinary Heroes: The Journal of a French Pioneer in Alberta.* Edmonton: University of Alberta Press, 1980.

Fournier, Martin. *Pierre-Esprit Radisson: Merchant, Adventurer, 1636–1710.* Québec: Septentrion, 2002.

Friesen, Gerald. *The Canadian Prairies: A History.* Toronto: University of Toronto Press, 1984.

Gagnon, François-Marc. *Jacques Cartier et la découverte du Nouveau Monde.* Québec: Musée du Québec, 1984.

Godbout, Arthur. *L'origine des écoles françaises dans l'Ontario.* Ottawa: Université d'Ottawa, 1972.

Gold, Gerald L. and Marc-Adelard Tremblay, eds. *Communities and Culture in French Canada.* Toronto: Holt, Rinehart and Winston, 1973.

Griffiths, Naomi E.S. *The Contexts of Acadian History, 1686–1784.* Published for the Centre for Canadian Studies, Mount Allison University. Montréal: McGill-Queen's Press, 1992.

Herb Belcourt. *Walking in the Woods: A Métis Journey.* Victoria: Brindle & Glass, 2006.

Jack Verney. *The Good Regiment: The Carignan-Salières Regiment in Canada, 1665–1668.* Montréal: McGill-Queen's University Press, 1992.

Johnson, Marc L. *The Winnipeg Francophone Community. Vitality Indicators for Official Language Minority Communities. Vol. 1: Francophones in Urban Settings.* Ottawa: Office of the Commissioner of Official Languages, 2007.

Krasnick Warsh, Cheryl, ed. *Drink in Canada: Historical Essays.* Montréal: McGill-Queen's University Press, 1993.

Le Blanc, Barbara. *Postcards from Acadie: Grand-Pre, Evangeline & the Acadian Identity.* Kentville, NS: Gaspereau, 2003.

Maxwell, Thomas R. *The Invisible French: The French in Metropolitan Toronto.* Waterloo: Wilfrid Laurier University Press, 1977.

Moogk, Peter N. *La Nouvelle France: The Making of French Canada, A Cultural History.* East Lansing: Michigan State University Press, 2000.

Morison, Samuel Eliot. *Samuel de Champlain, Father of New France.* Boston: Little, Brown and Company, 1972.

Morton, Desmond. *A Short History of Canada.* 2nd rev. ed. Toronto: McClelland & Stewart, 1994.

Noel, Janet. *Canada Dry: Temperance Crusades Before Confederation.* Toronto: University of Toronto Press, 1995.

Purkhardt, Brigitte. *La chasse-galerie, de la legende au myth: la symbolique du vol magique dans les recits québécois de chasse-galerie.* Montréal: XYZ, 1992.

Wardhaugh, Robert, ed. *Toward Defining the Prairies: Region, Culture, and History.* Winnipeg: University of Manitoba Press, 2001.

Weiss, Jonathan M. *French-Canadian Theater.* Boston: Twayne Publishers, 1986.

Woodcock, George. *Gabriel Dumont: The Metis Chief and his Lost World.* Peterborough: Broadview Press, 2003.

Young, Brian Jeffery. *George-Etienne Cartier: Montreal Bourgeois.* Montréal: McGill-Queen's University Press, 1981.

JULIE PERRONE

Julie Perrone is a historian currently completing her doctorate at Concordia University in Montréal. She is a member of the Institut d'histoire de l'Amérique française and the Canadian Historical Association. Born and raised in Montréal to a French-speaking family, Julie is raising her two sons to be fluent in both official languages. She also has a passion for sports, especially the Montréal Canadiens hockey club.